GAMBLING ACT 2005

EXPLANATORY NOTES

INTRODUCTION

1.   These explanatory notes relate to the Gambling Act 2005 (c.19). They have been prepared by the Department for Culture, Media and Sport. They do not form part of the Act and have not been endorsed by Parliament.

2.   These notes should be read in conjunction with the Act. They are not, and are not meant to be, a comprehensive description of the Act. Therefore, where a section or a part of a section does not seem to require any explanation or comment, none is given.

BACKGROUND

3.   The Gambling Act 2005 ("the Act") gives effect to the Government's proposals for reform of the law on gambling. The Act contains a new regulatory system to govern the provision of all gambling in Great Britain, other than the National Lottery and spread betting. The Act received royal assent on 7th April 2005. A table of references to Hansard, reproducing the proceedings for the passage of the Gambling Act through Parliament, is set out at the end of these notes.

4.   A draft Bill was published in November 2003 (Cm 6014), and further draft clauses were published in February and March 2004. The Bill followed on from the publication of a Government White Paper "A Safe Bet for Success" (Cm 5397) published in March 2002. The White Paper was itself the Government's response to the report of the Gambling Review Body (Cm 5206) published in July 2001. The purpose of the publication of the draft Bill was to enable pre-legislative scrutiny to take place, by a Joint Committee of both Houses. The Joint Committee was convened on 16th September 2003, and produced two reports on 7th April 2004 (HL paper 63-1; HC 139-1) and 22nd July 2004 (HL Paper 146-1; HC 843-1). The Government's responses to these reports were published on 14th June 2004 (Cm 6253) and 22nd September 2004 (Cm 6330).

SUMMARY OF THE ACT

5.   The Act repeals the Betting, Gaming and Lotteries Act 1963 (c.2), the Gaming Act 1968 (c.65) and the Lotteries and Amusements Act 1976 (c. 32).

6.   Gambling will be unlawful in Great Britain, unless permitted by:

- the measures contained in this Act; or

- measures contained in the National Lottery etc. Act 1993 (c.39), or pursuant to the Financial Services and Markets Act 2000 (c.8).

7.   Two comprehensive offences are established: providing facilities for gambling or using premises for gambling, in either case without the appropriate permission. Such permission may come from a licence, permit, or registration granted pursuant to the Act or from an exemption given by the Act. Where authority to provide facilities for gambling is obtained under the Act, it will be subject to varying degrees of regulation, depending on the type of gambling, the means by which it is conducted, and the people by whom and to whom it is offered.

8.   The Act introduces a unified regulator for gambling in Great Britain, the Gambling Commission ("the Commission"), and a new licensing regime for commercial gambling (to be conducted by the Commission or by licensing authorities, depending on the matter to be licensed). The Act removes from licensing justices all responsibility for granting gaming and betting permissions, which they exercised previously. Instead, the Commission and licensing authorities will share between them responsibility for all those matters previously regulated by licensing justices.

9.   The Commission will not regulate spread betting, which is currently the preserve of the Financial Services Authority (at least for the time being), or the National Lottery, which is regulated by the National Lottery Commission. Those aside, the Commission will regulate all commercial gambling in Great Britain.

10.   The Commission will take over from the Gaming Board for Great Britain. In addition to assuming responsibility for the Board's current remit of regulating gaming and certain lotteries, the Commission will take on responsibility for regulating betting. The Commission will be responsible for granting operating and personal licences for commercial gambling operators and personnel working in the industry. It will also regulate certain lottery managers and promoters. The Act sets out different types of operating licence that cover the full spectrum of commercial gambling activities conducted in Great Britain. It also makes provision for the Commission to have powers of entry and inspection to regulate gambling, with safeguards for those subject to the powers.

11.   The Act establishes a Gambling Appeals Tribunal to hear appeals from decisions made by the Commission.

12.   Licensing authorities will have new powers to license gambling premises within their area, as well as undertaking functions in relation to lower stake gaming machines and clubs and miners' welfare institutes. In England and Wales local authorities are given these responsibilities; in Scotland they are given to licensing boards. There will be a new system of temporary use notices. These will

authorise premises that are not licensed generally for gambling purposes to be used for certain types of gambling, for limited periods.

13.   The Act contains three licensing objectives which underpin the functions that the Commission and licensing authorities will perform. These objectives are central to the new regulatory regime created by the Act. They are:

- Protecting children and other vulnerable people from being harmed or exploited by gambling;
- Preventing gambling from being a source of crime or disorder, being associated with crime or disorder, or being used to support crime; and
- Ensuring that gambling is conducted in a fair and open way.

14.   Regulation of gambling in Great Britain will be achieved through a variety of measures established under the Act. These include:

- Secondary Legislation;
- Conditions on Licences;
- Codes of Practice; and
- Guidance.

15.   The Act recognises and accommodates the significant technological changes that have taken place in the last 40 years. The Act requires regulation of gambling where the player is not present on the operator's premises. For example, operators based in Great Britain must obtain an operating licence to authorise the provision of gambling via remote communication e.g. via interactive television or the internet. Moreover, the new licensing system has been designed to keep pace with technological developments, so that, subject to appropriate Parliamentary approval, gambling delivered by new, unforeseen, methods can be regulated in the future.

16.   The Act revises the law of gambling. For example commercial bingo premises and casinos will no longer have to operate as clubs with a 24 hour membership rule (making them places to which the public will now have access); and a new class of betting intermediary operating licence has been introduced, to cater for the development of betting exchanges. The Act also repeals legislation that has prevented contracts relating to gambling from being enforceable through the courts.

17.   The Act makes significant changes to the regime for casinos. It removes certain regulatory controls which existed under the Gaming Act 1968 (for example, "permitted" areas and the demand test). Three categories of casino are introduced (regional, large and small). These are defined according to a casino's size. A casino's category affects what forms of gambling can be provided at the casino. For example, a casino's gaming machine entitlement depends upon which category it falls into. There

will be a minimum size limit for new casinos established under the Act.

18.   The Act imposes an initial limit of 1 regional casino, and 8 small and 8 large casinos, to be licensed under the Act. There are powers to amend these limits or remove them entirely, subject to appropriate Parliamentary approval. Casinos which are in operation, or which can lawfully be operated, immediately before the casino provisions of the Act come into force will be allowed to continue to operate. This will be provided for by means of transitional provisions. A power is provided for licensing authorities to pass resolutions not to licence any new casinos premises in their area.

19.   The Act introduces a new regime for gaming machines. A new definition of gaming machine is provided, together with power to prescribe categories. The Act provides certain entitlements for commercial operators to use specified numbers and categories of machines in consequence of their licences. It also establishes permit procedures for authorising use of the lower stake gaming machines in specific locations.

20.   The Act provides protection for children and vulnerable adults from the effects of harmful gambling. It does this through a number of specific offences that will prevent children and young people from being given access to inappropriate or harmful gambling opportunities. In particular, it will be an offence to invite or permit a child or a young person to gamble contrary to the provisions of the Act. The Commission is required to promote socially responsible gambling through licence conditions and codes of practice directed at those providing facilities for gambling. The Act also provides powers for the Commission to void bets that are unfair, for example due to cheating.

21.   A revised regime for the law of lotteries is contained in the Act, building upon that contained in the Lotteries and Amusements Act 1976, which the Act repeals. The Act regulates lotteries in two ways: either as exempt lotteries, or as licensable lotteries.

22.   The Act makes provision for the advertising of gambling, creating new offences relating to the advertising of unlawful gambling and providing powers for the Secretary of State to make regulations controlling the content of gambling advertisements.

23.   The Act establishes a series of authorisations for private and non-commercial gambling in Great Britain. This includes authorisations for domestic gaming and betting, and provisions for gaming and lotteries at non-commercial events.

STRUCTURE OF THE ACT

24.   The Act is set out as follows:

- Part 1, and Schedules 1 and 2 introduce the fundamental concepts used in the Act, including definitions for "gambling", "betting", "gaming", "lottery" "casino", "remote gambling" and "licensing authorities". Part 1 also makes provision for situations where activities may fall into more than one category of gambling, and ensures that the forms of gambling regulated by the Act do not generally include entering a lottery forming part of the National Lottery. Schedule 3 makes amendments to the National Lottery etc. Act 1993.

- Part 2, and Schedules 4 and 5 establish the Gambling Commission, define its powers and give effect to the transfer from the Gaming Board of Great Britain. The core powers and duties of the Commission are set out, including its consultation obligations.

- Part 3 sets out the general offences, including two key offences: the unlawful provision of facilities for gambling and the unlawful use of premises for gambling. Part 3 also makes provision for the prohibition of "chain gifting schemes", a revised offence of cheating, and provisions on the manufacture of gambling software.

- Part 4 establishes a number of specific offences that involve the participation of children and young people in gambling, their employment in relation to gambling and their entry to premises licensed to provide gambling.

- Part 5 and Schedule 7 concern operating licences issued by the Commission. This Part establishes:

  - The different types of licence and the rules relating to them;
  - The conditions which may be attached to them;
  - The required procedure for applying for them;
  - The requirements as to their duration and validity; and
  - A review procedure, including powers to revoke licenses and impose financial penalties.
- Part 5 also provides powers for the raising of a levy on operating licence holders.

- Part 6 concerns personal licences issued by the Commission. It defines the circumstances in which the Commission can impose requirements upon a person to hold a personal licence, and the procedures and rules relating to personal licences.

- Part 7 and Schedule 8 create a tribunal to hear appeals from decisions taken by the Commission and provide the relevant powers and procedures for bringing an appeal. It includes powers to be exercised by the Lord Chancellor.

- Part 8 concerns premises licences issued by licensing authorities. This Part describes the functions of licensing authorities, the various types of premises licence and the procedures for application. It sets out powers for licensing authorities and the Secretary of State or Scottish Ministers to attach conditions to licences. There are provisions on the duration, transfer and review of licences, and the mechanisms by which appeals can be made.

- Part 8 also contains provisions for determining limits on the number of casino premises licences which may be granted under the Act. Schedule 9 makes provision for dealing with applications where such limits are in place.

- Part 9 provides a procedure for authorising the temporary use of non-gambling premises for gambling. Licensing authorities are responsible for these authorisations, which are time limited.

- Part 10 and Schedule 10 provide a new framework of regulation for gaming machines. There is power for the Secretary of State to prescribe categories of machine, by reference to the levels of charge and prize, the nature of the prize or the gambling, and the premises where the machine is to be located. Manufacture and supply of a gaming machine will require an operating licence from the Commission, and making a gaming machine available for use without the necessary permission is an offence.

- Part 11 and Schedule 11 establish a new regime for lotteries, which is based upon, but revises the regime set out in the Lotteries and Amusements Act 1976. Part 5 also contains provisions for licensing lotteries. A new category of lawful lottery, the customer lottery, is created in Schedule 11. There are a number of new rules concerning the operation and promotion of lotteries.

- Part 12 and Schedule 12 establish a new regime for gambling in clubs and miners' welfare institutes, developed from the regime in the Gaming Act 1968. It makes provision for the grant of permits by licensing authorities where gaming exceeds certain levels or where it involves the provision of gaming machines. There is also a requirement for bingo operating licences to be obtained, where the size of the bingo games played exceeds a specified threshold.

- Part 12 and Schedule 13 make provision for gaming and gaming machines in premises holding an alcohol licence. Part 12 is also concerned with the use of gaming machines at travelling fairs.

- Part 13 and Schedule 14 make provision for prize gaming which is to be permitted in certain locations, subject to specific rules.

- Part 14 and Schedule 15 make provision for private and non-commercial gambling, which the Act authorises without any requirement for further permission.

- Part 15 deals with the inspection rights and powers that are needed by the police, Commission enforcement officers, and local authority officers so that they can carry out their functions under the Act. Safeguards are afforded to those who may be the subject of inspection.

- Part 16 provides a new regime for the advertising of gambling, replacing a number of provisions spread across different pieces of legislation, which the Act repeals. It creates new offences relating to the advertising of unlawful and foreign gambling, and provides powers for the Secretary of State to make regulations controlling the advertising of gambling.

- Part 17 makes new provision for contracts relating to gambling. It repeals a number of statutes, dating from the eighteenth and nineteenth centuries, which prevented gambling contracts from being enforceable at law. It also makes provision for contracts relating to bets to be made void in circumstances where the Commission believes the bet was unfair, in particular as a result of misuse of information or cheating.

- Part 18 provides an interpretation section and a number of general provisions applicable to the Act as a whole. Part 18 and Schedule 6 also provide powers for the Commission to exchange information with other bodies in the exercise of their functions.

- Part 18 and Schedule 18 give the Secretary of State power to make regulations to provide for the transition from the old regime for gambling regulation to the new regime established by the Act.

- Schedules 16 and 17 provide for consequential amendments to other legislation and for repeals as a result of the Act.

TERRITORIAL EXTENT

25.   The Act generally extends to England and Wales, and to Scotland with the exception of sections 148 (legal assistance scheme), 221 (fees) and 346 (prosecution by licensing authority). Sections 43 (chain gift schemes), 331 (foreign gambling) and 340 (foreign betting) apply to Northern Ireland.

Territorial application: Wales
26.   The Act's effect in Wales is the same as in England. The Act contains no provisions that relate exclusively to Wales, or affect the National Assembly for Wales.

Territorial application: Scotland
27.   The Act's effect in Scotland is the same as in England, with the exception of the following sections:

- sections 148 (legal assistance scheme), 212 (fees) and 346 (prosecution by licensing authority) are not applicable in Scotland;

- sections 151 (form of licence), 159 (making of application), 160 (notice of application), 161 (representation), 164 and 165 (grant and rejection of application), 167 (mandatory conditions), 168 (default conditions), 184 (annual fee), 190 (copy of licence), 197 and 200 (review), 219 (giving notice), 349 (three-year licensing policy), and paragraphs (5)(d) of Schedule 10 (FEC permits) and 6(e) and 21(2) of Schedule 14 (prize gaming permits) provide

Scottish Ministers with the power to make their own regulations in respect of premises licence and permit matters in Scotland;

- section 285 (clubs, pubs etc.: special provision for Scotland) enables Scottish Ministers, with the consent of the Secretary of State, to make provision by regulations in respect of club gaming and machine permits in place of that in Schedule 12; and in respect of licensed premises gaming machine permits in place of that in Schedule 13; and

- sections 33 (provision of facilities for gambling), 37 (use of premises), 41 (gambling software), 42 (cheating), 43 (chain gift schemes), 62 (penalty), 139 (breach of personal licence condition), 246 (penalty), 263 (penalty), 301 (misusing profits of non-commercial prize gaming), 328 (regulations), 330 (unlawful gambling), 331 (foreign gambling), 342 (false information) and 345 (forfeiture) make provision for a term of imprisonment on summary conviction not to exceed 51 weeks. The application of these sections to Scotland differs in that the maximum term of imprisonment is 6 months.

- Section 155 (delegation of functions under Part 8: Scotland) contains particular provisions regarding the delegation arrangements within licensing boards for functions conferred under the Act.

Territorial limits – vessels and aircraft

28.   Sections 359 and 360 contain provisions for determining the territorial extent of the Act in relation to vessels and aircraft.

PART 1: INTERPRETATION OF KEY CONCEPTS

29.   Part 1 sets out definitions for the most important expressions and concepts that run through the Act. Part 18 also contains an interpretation section.

Section 1: The licensing objectives

30.   The Act sets out licensing functions to be exercised by the Commission in relation to operating and personal licences, and by licensing authorities in relation to the licensing of premises and the grant of certain permits. In exercising these functions, the Commission and licensing authorities must be guided by the licensing objectives, which underpin the new regulatory regime. The licensing objectives for the Act are:

- Preventing gambling from being a source of crime or disorder, being associated with crime or disorder or being used to support crime;

- Ensuring that gambling is conducted in a fair and open way; and

- Protecting children and other vulnerable people from being harmed or exploited by gambling.

Section 2: Licensing authorities

31.   This section defines the term "licensing authority" and therefore determines who is to discharge the licensing authority's functions under the Act. These functions include the licensing of gambling premises under Parts 8 and 9; the issue of permits authorising gaming and gaming machines in other premises under Parts 10, 12 and 13; and the registration of certain lotteries under Part 11. In England and Wales, local authorities are to act as the licensing authority for the purposes of the Act.   In Scotland, licensing authorities are to be licensing boards constituted under section 1 of the Licensing (Scotland) Act 1976 (c.66).

32.   The definition of "licensing authority" mirrors that in the Licensing Act 2003 (c.17), omitting (except in relation to the provisions of Part 12 governing gaming and gaming machines in alcohol-licensed premises) certain bodies who should have functions only in relation to the subject matter of that Act. This will allow licensing authorities in England and Wales to coordinate their functions in relation to alcohol licensing and the licensing of gambling premises, as is already possible in Scotland. Part 8 makes further provision to achieve this.

33.   Although there is no specific reference to a "metropolitan council" or a "unitary council" in the list of licensing authorities, these councils are types of district or county council and are therefore already covered in the list.

Section 3: Gambling

34.   This section defines "gambling" as meaning betting, gaming and participating in a lottery (within the meaning of those expressions as defined in subsequent provisions of Part 1). This is the first time that legislation has provided a generic concept of gambling, of which gaming, betting and lotteries are specific kinds. The Act adopts the approach recommended by the Gambling Review Body that there should be a single regulatory system for gambling, with different and distinctive provision for any of its specific forms, as appropriate. Accordingly, a definition of "gambling" is provided which defines the forms of gambling which are to be brought within the system of regulation set out in the Act, and distinguishes them from activities which, although they combine expenditure and the influence of chance, should not be treated as gambling for the purposes of regulation.

Section 4: Remote gambling

35.   The Act contains specific provisions concerned with the regulation of the various technological means by which gambling activities can now be conducted. The Act adopts the concept of "remote gambling" to cover gambling where the participants are not face to face on the same premises.

36.   This section defines "remote gambling" to mean gambling where people are participating by means of "remote communication".   The types of remote communication by which people may participate in remote gambling are:

- the internet;

- telephone;

- television;

- radio; or

- any other kind of electronic or other technology for facilitating communication.

37.   This list encompasses modern means of communication such as interactive television and mobile telephony, and is able, by virtue of *subsection (2)(e),* to ensure that the definition keeps pace with future developments in this field. However, in order to ensure clarity as well as flexibility for the regulation of gambling, the Secretary of State may specify in regulations that a specified system or method of communication is, or is not, to be treated as a form of remote communication for the purpose of the definition.

Section 5: Facilities for gambling
38.   The fundamental concept in the Act is the provision of facilities for gambling. It underpins the offences in Parts 3 and 4, and the requirements for licensing in Parts 5, 6 and 8. There are many ways in which individuals and organisations can provide gambling activities, or take part in them, whether through remote communication or in more traditional ways. This section defines the activities which are subject to regulation under the Act.

39.   *Subsection (1)* sets out the circumstances in which a person is to be treated as providing facilities for gambling.

40.   The list in *paragraphs (a) to (c)* of subsection (1) is aimed at different levels and aspects of the operation of gambling. Paragraph (a) is aimed at people and companies who are in the business of providing gambling. Any person who offers the opportunity for people to gamble, whether at a casino or licensed betting premises or through a website, will expressly or by implication be inviting people to gamble in accordance with arrangements made by them.

41.   In paragraph (b), the reference to providing arrangements for gambling carries a general flavour of causing facilities to be available. The reference to operating arrangements for gambling is apt for mechanical arrangements such as a roulette wheel. Administering arrangements for gambling is a wide concept carrying a general flavour of control.

42.   Paragraph (c) is concerned with those people who are directly involved in the gambling operation itself. People who participate in the operation of gambling by others will include those who actually play a part in the gambling transaction. An example might be a croupier at a gaming table. People who participate in the administration of gambling will include those who, whilst they do not actually operate the gambling, nevertheless provide direct administrative back-up to the gambling transaction. An example would be a person who hands out betting slips for the

completion of a betting transaction.

43.   *Subsection (2)* restricts the scope of subsection (1) by providing for certain exceptions. The exceptions cover:

- the supply of goods (other than a gaming machine) to a person who intends to use them to provide facilities for gambling (*paragraph (a)*), e.g. the supplier of gaming chips to a casino;

- the supply of goods to a person who may use them for gambling (but not where the supply is in the course of any of the activities referred to in subsection (1)(b) or (c)) (*paragraph (b)*), e.g. a retailer supplying a pack of playing cards to a person for domestic use; and

- electronic communications providers who do nothing more than act as a carrier of information for people providing facilities for gambling or consumers partaking in gambling (*paragraph (c)*), e.g. an internet service provider or mobile telephone operator.

44.   *Subsection (3)* sets out the circumstances in which, despite the exception in subsection (2)(c), making available a means of remote communication will be providing facilities for gambling under the Act. This will be so where, because of the way in which the facilities have been adapted or presented, either they cannot reasonably be expected to be used for purposes other than gambling, or they are intended to be used wholly or mainly for gambling. This might include, for example, where an internet connected personal computer is adapted so that it has a home page menu dedicated to providing links to gambling websites. It would also cover the situation where an internet connected personal computer was surrounded by signs indicating that it was available for use for gambling, and giving details of specific web pages where gambling was available.

45.   *Subsection (4)* adds to the provision in subsection (3). It confers an order making power on the Secretary of State to clarify those cases where facilities for remote communication can or cannot reasonably be expected to be used for purposes other than gambling; or where facilities are to be taken as being intended, or not intended, to be used wholly or mainly for gambling.

Section 6: Gaming and game of chance
46.   This section defines "gaming" for the purposes of the Act as playing a game of chance for a prize, and then further defines the meaning of a "game of chance" and the concept of playing. The definitions are based on the relevant provisions in section 52 of the Gaming Act 1968, revised for the requirements of the Act. In particular, *subsection (3)* provides that a person can play a game of chance even if there are no other players, or the actions of a computer stand in for another player. This ensures that gaming on a machine or with virtual games is brought within the scope of the Act.

47. *Subsection (6)* provides the Secretary of State with the power to prescribe whether a particular activity (or an activity carried on in specified circumstances) does or does not amount to:

- a game;

- a game of chance; or

- a sport,

for the purpose of defining gaming under this section. The purpose of subsection (6) is to cater for circumstances, which might arise in the future, where either a new product or activity is introduced and there is doubt as to its treatment under this section, or where the interpretation being given to this section means it would be prudent to put beyond doubt the proper classification of a particular activity in relation to the definition of gaming.

Section 7: Casino
48. This section provides a statutory definition of a "casino" for the first time in British law.

49. The definition establishes that a casino is an arrangement (whether on premises or via remote communication such as the internet) where people can participate in casino games. *Subsection (2)* defines "casino games" as games which are not equal chance games. This means that any games which involve playing or staking against a bank, or where the chances are not equally favourable to all the players, will be casino games.

50. *Subsection (3)* enables the Secretary of State to provide in regulations for a specified activity to be, or not to be, treated as a casino game for the purposes of the definition of casino. This power is not the same as specifying what kinds of casino games (e.g. roulette or blackjack) may be played in a licensed casino. Separate powers to specify such matters are provided in Part 5 on operating licences, specifically section 90.

51. The Act regulates casinos in different ways, depending on their size and the facilities they provide. *Subsection (5)* provides for four categories of casino, to be defined in regulations made by the Secretary of State; and *subsection (6)* specifically enables casinos to be classified by reference to a number of different matters. These include:

- the number of gaming tables at which casino games (or classes of casino games) are made available;

- the location and concentration of gaming tables; and

- the use and designation of floor areas for particular purposes.

52.   In making such regulations, the Secretary of State can include provisions for determining what is and is not to be treated as a gaming table for the purposes of the casino definition, and for calculating when a floor area is to be treated as being used or designated for a particular purpose (see *subsection (7)*).

53.   The three categories of casino to be licensed under the Act are: regional, large, and small. A regional casino will have the largest floor space requirements, followed by large casinos, and then small casinos. There is a fourth class of casino, which is a casino below the minimum size for a licensed casino (subsection (5)(d)). Casinos which have been licensed under the Gaming Act 1968, and which are too small to comply with the minimum requirements specified for regional, large or small casinos will fall into this fourth category. Transitional arrangements, under Part 18 of the Act, will be made to permit this fourth class of casino to continue in operation.

54.   The Regulatory Impact Assessment published alongside the Act contains full details of the proposed specifications for regional, large and small casinos.

55.   Sections 90, 166, 174, 175, 176 and Schedule 9, while not an exhaustive list, all contain particular provisions relevant to the regulation of casinos under the Act.

Section 8: Equal chance gaming
56.   Under the Gaming Act 1968, the distinction is drawn between games of equal chance and games of unequal chance (including bankers' games). The Act maintains this distinction, and offers different degrees of regulation and control depending on which types of facilities for gaming are being offered. This section provides a definition of equal chance gaming.

57.   At a number of places in the Act rights to conduct equal chance gaming are granted. See, for example, Part 12 on clubs, and the provisions of Part 14 on private and non-commercial gaming. By contrast, unequal chance gaming or bankers' games may only be made available, under the Act, in limited circumstances, the main example being that of a licensed casino.

Section 9: Betting: general
58.   This section defines "betting" for the purposes of the Act. The present law contains no statutory definition of "betting" as an activity. In broad terms it is taken to mean the staking of money or other value on the outcome of a doubtful issue. Betting can be at fixed odds, by means of a spread, or by way of pool betting.

59.   By virtue of this section (which is subject to the qualification in Section 10) betting covers making, accepting or negotiating a bet in relation to:

- the outcome of any race, competition or event,
- the likelihood of anything occurring or not occurring, or

- whether something is true or not.

60.   *Subsections (2) and (3)* extend the meaning of the term to include bets on races, competitions, or events that have occurred in the past.

Section 10: Spread bets &c.

61.   Spread bets or other bets, which are subject to regulation under section 22 of the Financial Services and Markets Act 2000, are excluded from the definition of betting in this Part. Section 22 of the 2000 Act provides for regulated activities under that Act to be specified in an order. The relevant order is the Financial Services and Markets Act 2000 (Regulated Activities) Order 2001 (S.I. 2001/544). Article 85 of that Order specifies as a regulated activity investments in rights under:

- a contract for differences, or

- any other contracts the purpose or pretended purpose of which is to secure a profit or avoid a loss by reference to fluctuations in the price or value of property, or fluctuations in an index or other factor specified in the contract,

and spread bets are accepted as falling within this description.

62.   If a class of bet ceases to be subject to such regulation as a result of an order under section 22 of that Act, it automatically becomes subject to regulation under the Act. *Subsection (2)* enables transitional provisions to be included in any such order under section 22 to ensure that the switch to regulation under the Act happens in an orderly way.

Section 11: Betting: prize competitions

63.   Schemes purporting to be prize competitions will fall within the definition of betting in this Part, even though they may not involve the deposit of a stake in the way normal to betting, if they satisfy specified conditions. One of the conditions is a requirement to pay to enter; and Schedule 1 defines what amounts to "payment to enter".

64.   The effect of making such schemes subject to regulation as betting is to ensure that all the relevant protections provided by the Act in respect of betting apply. Therefore, schemes such as "fantasy football" competitions or the Racing Post's "Ten to Follow" competition will be regulated in the same way as bets placed on single events. However, the definition is intended to exclude prize competitions (such as prize crosswords) where the elements of prediction and wagering are not both present.

Section 12: Pool betting

65.   This section defines "pool betting". It is based on the definition in section 10 of the Betting and Gaming Duties Act 1981 (c.63), and has been amended to remove those various elements which are no longer relevant to the definition for the purposes of the Act.

Section 13: Betting intermediary

66.   A person who provides a service for others to make or accept bets is called a "betting intermediary" in the Act. Such a person does not, himself, partake in the bet. The definition includes betting exchanges. There is a separate class of operating licence for betting intermediaries.

Section 14: Lottery

67.   This section provides a definition of a lottery. It is intended to give statutory effect to the broad definition which the courts have evolved over recent years, while making specific additional provision in relation to arrangements whose status under the current law has proved problematic or uncertain.

68.   The definition of lottery recognises that a lottery may involve more than one process for determining who the prize winners are. Where an arrangement involves more than one process then it fulfils the definition of a lottery if the first of those processes relies wholly on chance; and this is so even if subsequent processes require the lottery entrant to exercise skill or judgment. Conversely, where the first of these processes does not rely wholly on chance, the arrangement will not be a lottery, even if subsequent processes do not require any skill or judgment to be exercised whatsoever.

69.   An arrangement will only be a lottery if the participants are required to pay to enter. Schedule 2 gives further detail on what amounts to "payment to enter" for the purposes of this section.

70.   The definition of lottery also contains provisions which replace section 14 of the Lotteries and Amusements Act 1976. Section 14 of that Act made provision about the level of skill required for a legal prize competition. There is no direct equivalent of section 14 in this Act. Instead, competitions that do not require a minimum level of skill (according to the test in *subsection (5)*) are treated as relying wholly on chance, and therefore fall within the definition of a lottery (provided the other elements of the definition are satisfied).

71.   Genuine prize competitions are not prohibited. So, under subsection (5), a process is not to be treated as relying wholly on chance if it contains a requirement to exercise skill and judgement, or knowledge that is reasonably likely to:

    a) prevent a significant proportion of people who wish to participate from doing so; or

    b) prevent a significant proportion of people who participate from receiving a prize.

72.   If either one of these barriers to entry or success can be shown, the process will not be deemed to rely wholly on chance, and the arrangement will not be a lottery.

73.   The test in subsection (5) is intended to be a practical one. So, for example, the level of skill or judgement required to win or go forward to the next round in a children's competition should be set at an appropriate level for the age of the children at which the competition is aimed. Equally, a competition in a specialist magazine needs to be suitably challenging for the specialists likely to read the magazine and enter the competition. The requirements of subsection (5) are not, therefore, necessarily satisfied by requiring a level of skill or judgment that could be expected to challenge the public at large.

74.   *Subsection (7)* gives the Secretary of State power to provide in regulations whether a particular arrangement or a particular kind of arrangement is, or is not, to be treated as a lottery. The purpose of subsection (7) is to cater for circumstances which might arise in the future, such as where a new product or activity is introduced and there is doubt as to its treatment under this section. This enables the matter to be put beyond doubt.

Section 15: National Lottery
75.   This section ensures that participating in lotteries forming part of the National Lottery is not regulated as gambling under the Act. This is subject to two exceptions: section 42, which creates the offence of cheating; and section 335, which concerns the enforceability of gambling contracts.

Section 16: Betting and gaming
76.   Gambling transactions where there is an overlap between betting and gaming will be treated as gaming for the purposes of the Act, unless the betting in question constitutes pool betting. This ensures, amongst other things, that activities which are available in licensed gaming premises are not also available on licensed betting premises because, like roulette, they involve placing bets.

Section 17: Lotteries and gaming
77.   Where gambling transactions satisfy the definitions of both games of chance and lotteries, then the arrangements fall under the controls on gaming unless they constitute a lawful lottery. The exception to this rule is transactions that require a person to participate, or be successful, in more than three processes. In that case, regardless of whether the transaction satisfies the definition of a lottery, it is always gaming. This broadly maintains the position in the current law (section 52 of the Gaming Act 1968).

Section 18: Lotteries and betting
78.   Transactions that satisfy both:

- the definition of pool betting or a betting prize competition, and

- the definition of entering a lottery,

are to be treated as betting unless they form part of a lawful lottery. This section does not apply to lotteries forming part of the National Lottery which are excluded from being betting for the purposes of the Act by section 15(4).

Section 19: Non-commercial society

79.   This section defines the circumstances in which a society is to be treated as non-commercial for the purposes of Part 11 and Schedule 11. It also contains the definition of "private gain" for the purpose of Part 14.

80.   Societies that are established for cultural or sporting purposes are deemed to be non-commercial societies under *subsection (1)*. This is so, even if they provide benefits to individuals (*subsection (3)*).

81.   Societies other than those with charitable or sporting purposes will only be non-commercial if their purposes are for something other than private gain. Therefore, these societies will be considered commercial, if their purpose is to provide benefit to a particular individual or individuals.

82.   To illustrate, genuine societies that are set up to provide a child with medical care or sports sponsorship are likely to be non-commercial societies under this section. However, a society set up for political purposes would need to be set up to promote the party or group as a whole, rather than to have as its purpose the payment of sums to the benefit of particular individuals, for their own benefit.

Schedule 1: Betting: prize competitions: definition of payment to enter

83.   Schedule 1 defines the circumstances in which someone is to be treated as having to pay to participate for the purposes of the "betting: prize competitions" definition in section 11. The definition covers cases where a participant has to send money (or its equivalent), and also transferring money's worth and paying for goods and services at a price or rate which reflects the opportunity to participate in the prize competition.

84.   Entry by standard rate telephone call, ordinary post (such as ordinary first class post) or by the use of another comparable service at its standard price to submit an entry, or to claim a prize, is not to be regarded as payment for entry.

85.   Where an operator or any third party earns income from the prize competition because an entrant has to pay to discover whether a prize has been won or to take possession of the prize (for example, by means of a premium rate telephone line), then this is to be treated as payment to participate.

86.   A prize competition is not to be regarded as requiring payment for entry, provided that a free entry route is offered for the competition (for example, a letter sent by ordinary post or another method of communication which is neither more expensive or less convenient than participating by paying). However, to qualify, the free entry route must be displayed with equal prominence as the other means of paid entry, and entries which are not paid for must be no less likely to win all or any of the

prizes than entries which are paid for.

87.   The Schedule confers a power on the Secretary of State to make regulations which determine whether or not a specified arrangement is to count as requiring payment to participate. New schemes and kinds of competition are always being devised; and this power will enable any uncertainty which might arise about payment to be resolved in the regulations.

Schedule 2: Lotteries: definition of payment to enter

88.   Part 1 contains the definition of a lottery for the purposes of the Act. The definition consists of three elements, one of which is that people are required to pay to enter the lottery. Schedule 2 sets out what is meant by payment to enter for the purposes of a lottery. The provisions of this Schedule closely follow those in Schedule 1 for prize competitions.

89.   It will not be possible for an operator to circumvent the provisions on payment to enter, explained above in relation to Schedule 1, by providing two methods of entry, both of which are communication at a premium rate, or one of which is a payment and the other is communication at a premium rate. This is because any method of communication that is charged at above the normal rate (i.e. at a rate that reflects the opportunity to enter the lottery) is deemed to be "payment" under *paragraph 2(c)*. So, where there is a choice between payment to enter, and entry through, say, a premium rate telephone line, there is no choice of free entry under *paragraph 8*, and both methods constitute payment. The arrangement will therefore be a lottery.

Schedule 3: Amendment of the National Lottery etc. Act 1993 (c.39)

90.   Schedule 3 amends the National Lottery etc. Act 1993. It inserts a new provision in the 1993 Act which will allow the Secretary of State to make regulations providing for the holders of licences under Part 1 of that Act to pay an annual levy to the Gambling Commission. The provision is based on that for operating licence holders under section 123 of the Act, and is subject to the condition that a levy will only be imposed where regulations have also been made under that section for a levy on operating licence holders. Schedule 3 also amends the 1993 Act to require the National Lottery Commission to consult the Gambling Commission where it becomes aware of any matter about which the Commission is likely to have an opinion, or where directed to do so by the Secretary of State.

PART 2: THE GAMBLING COMMISSION

91.   The Act creates a new, unified regulator for betting, gaming and lotteries in Great Britain called the Gambling Commission ("the Commission").

Section 20: Establishment of the Commission

92.   This section establishes the Commission, which will be the central regulatory

body for gambling in Great Britain. Schedule 4, explained below, sets out the constitution of the Commission and its proceedings, the appointment of Commissioners and staff, as well as its financial and reporting arrangements.

Section 21: Gaming Board: transfer to Commission

93.   The Commission will take over from the Gaming Board of Great Britain, which was established under the Gaming Act 1968 and currently regulates gaming and certain types of lotteries. When commenced, this section, and Schedule 5, will transfer the Gaming Board's functions, rights and liabilities (including property) to the Commission. This section also provides for the chairman and members of the Gaming Board in post immediately before the establishment of the Commission to become chairman and commissioners in the new organisation.

Section 22: Duty to promote the licensing objectives

94.   In carrying out its functions under the Act, the Commission must aim to pursue, and, wherever appropriate, have regard to the licensing objectives (as defined in section 1) and must aim to permit gambling in so far as it thinks such permission is reasonably consistent with pursuit of those objectives. Therefore, in carrying out its licensing functions under Parts 5 and 6 of the Act, or in issuing guidance and codes of practice or advising the Secretary of State in accordance with Part 2, the Commission will have regard to the licensing objectives.

Section 23: Policy for licensing and regulation

95.   Once established, the Commission will be responsible for licensing gambling operators and personnel working in the gambling industry under the provisions of Part 5 (operating licences) and Part 6 (personal licences) of the Act. This will be the primary licensing activity of the Commission, although the Act also provides it with other regulatory and advisory functions concerned with the proper conduct and control of gambling in Great Britain. The Commission will have investigation, enforcement and prosecution powers.

96.   This section requires the Commission to prepare, publish, and keep under review, a statement that sets out the principles which will govern the exercise of its functions, and, in particular, explain how such principles will assist the Commission in its pursuit of the licensing objectives. This statement will underpin the work of the Commission.

97.   Examples of specific matters for inclusion in the statement are: the principles, practice and procedure which the Commission will apply in considering applications for operating and personal licences under Parts 5 and 6.

98.   Before issuing or revising a statement, *subsection (5)* provides that the Commission must consult the following:

- The Secretary of State;

- Representatives of local authorities (including, in Scotland, licensing boards);

- Representatives of Chief Constables of police forces;

- Representatives of gambling businesses;

- Commissioners of Customs and Excise;

- People with knowledge of social problems that may be associated with gambling; and

- The public, to such and extent, and in such a way as it thinks appropriate.

99. The statement and any revisions to the statement must be published.

Section 24: Codes of practice

100. This section requires the Commission, as part of its regulatory functions, to publish codes of practice about the manner in which facilities for gambling are provided. These may be directed at the holders of operating or personal licences, or any other person involved in providing facilities for gambling. In particular, the Commission is required to publish a social responsibility code, which should describe the arrangements which a person providing facilities for gambling is to make for:

- ensuring that gambling is conducted in a fair and open way,

- protecting children and other vulnerable persons from harm or exploitation, and

- making help available to those who are, or may be, affected by problems related to gambling.

101. The Commission is required to publish its codes of practice, and all revisions, in a way that will ensure that those to whom they are addressed are made aware of them. A code, and any revision thereto, must state clearly when it is to come into effect. The Commission has the ability to revoke codes at any time.

102. Under Part 5, an operating licence is subject to the condition that the licensee complies with any relevant provision of a social responsibility code. Furthermore, it is open to the Commission to attach general or individual conditions to a licence requiring compliance with a provision of any other code (as further provided under Part 5). The same applies in relation to the Secretary of State's power to attach conditions to an operating licence.

103. A failure to comply with a code will not, of itself, render a person liable to prosecution or civil action. However, the codes can be used as evidence for criminal or civil proceedings; are to be taken into account by a court or tribunal in any case where it appears relevant; and are to be taken into account by the Commission in exercising any of its functions. For example, where a licence holder has his operating licence reviewed by the Commission for potential breach of a licence condition, under the powers provided in Part 5, the Commission will refer to a code of practice, where

it is relevant.

104.   Before issuing a code of practice, *subsection (10)* requires the Commission to consult:

- The Secretary of State;

- People with knowledge of social problems that may be associated with gambling;

- Commissioners of Customs and Excise;

- People who appear to the Commission to represent gambling businesses, which are likely to be affected by the code or revision; and

- Where a provision in a code is about the advertising of facilities for gambling, people who appear to the Commission to have a relevant responsibility for regulating the advertising industry.

105.   *Subsection (11)* requires the Commission to consult the following people as well, but only to the extent that it thinks it appropriate depending on the context and subject matter of the code:

- Representatives of local authorities (including, in Scotland, licensing boards);

- Representatives of Chief Constables of police forces;

- Representatives of gambling businesses other than mandatory consultees under subsection (10) (such as, those persons who are unlikely to be directly affected by the code); and

- The public (in such a manner as the Commission thinks fit).

106.   The references to consultation of local authorities in sections 23 and 24 are to be read in the wider context, and includes parts of a local authority other than that responsible for licensing matters. This is to ensure that relevant parts of local government (in England, Scotland, and Wales) are consulted, where appropriate, in respect of the Commission's policy statement and codes of practice.

Section 25: Guidance to local authorities
107.   Under the Act, licensing authorities (local authorities in England and Wales, licensing boards in Scotland, and, where applicable, the Sub-Treasurer of the Inner Temple and the Under-Treasurer of the Middle Temple) are required to undertake various regulatory functions in relation to a number of gambling activities. They are responsible for:

- licensing of premises for gambling activities (Parts 8 and 9);

- regulating members' clubs and miners' welfare institutes which wish to undertake certain gaming activities (Part 12 and Schedule 12);

- regulating gaming and gaming machines in premises licensed to supply alcohol under the Licensing Act 2003. This includes granting licensed premises gaming machine permits (Part 12 and Schedule 13);

- granting permits to family entertainment centres for the use of certain lower stake gaming machines (Part 10 and Schedule 10);

- granting permits for prize gaming (Part 13 and Schedule 14); and

- registering societies' lotteries which fall below certain prescribed thresholds (Schedule 11, Part 5).

108.   In order to assist licensing authorities to perform these various licensing and regulatory functions, this section requires the Commission to issue and publish guidance about how licensing authorities are to exercise their functions under the Act, including the principles to be applied in exercising those functions.

109.   Licensing authorities are under a duty to have regard to such guidance.

110.   Before issuing guidance to licensing authorities, *subsection (4)* requires the Commission to consult:

- The Secretary of State,

- The Scottish Ministers,

- Commissioners of Customs and Excise,

- Representatives of local authorities (as defined by this section),

- Representatives of gambling businesses, and

- People with knowledge of social problems that may be associated with gambling.

111.   Depending on the nature of the code, or any revision, *subsection (5)* also requires the Commission to consult if, and to the extent it thinks it appropriate to do so:

- Representatives of Chief Constables of police forces; and

- Members of the public (in such a manner as the Commission thinks fit).

Section 26: Duty to advise the Secretary of State
112.   One of the functions of the Commission is to provide advice to the Secretary of State on matters relating to gambling as described in this section. This section permits the Commission to give advice about gambling to the Secretary of State either in response to a request or on its own initiative. Copies of any such advice will be sent to the Scottish Ministers also.

Section 27: Compliance

113. This section gives the Commission power to undertake activities for the purpose of assessing compliance with the provisions of the Act, or whether an offence has been committed under the Act. In particular, the Commission will be able to use children and young persons in test purchasing activities to assess whether the provisions for prevention of under-age gambling in Part 4 of the Act are being complied with. Section 64 exempts children, and people acting in the course of their duty, from committing an offence in these circumstances.

Section 28: Investigation and prosecution of offences

114. The Commission has the power to investigate whether an offence has been committed under the Act, and to pursue criminal proceedings if this is the case. The Commission can do this on its own initiative or acting on other information. The power for the Commission <u>itself</u> to bring criminal proceedings does not apply in Scotland, due to the particular requirements of the criminal justice system in that jurisdiction.

Section 29: Licensing authority information

115. Under the Act, Commission and licensing authorities must maintain registers containing appropriate details of licences that they have each issued. These registers will be open to the public. There will be circumstances where the Commission will need to obtain information directly from licensing authorities. For example, such information may be needed by the Commission to fulfil its duty under this Part to advise the Secretary of State. This section places an obligation on licensing authorities to comply with requests from the Commission for information contained in a register maintained by the authority, or for information in the authority's possession in consequence of their licensing and regulatory functions.

Section 30: Other exchange of information

116. This section permits the Commission to pass on information received in the course of its functions to those people or organisations listed in Parts 1 and 2 of Schedule 6, for use in the course of their, or the Commission's, business. This section also provides a reciprocal power for the bodies listed in the Schedule to provide information to the Commission. Conditions may be imposed where information is provided under this section. The Commission may also provide information to the Comptroller and Auditor General for use in the exercise of his functions or to a person for use in a criminal investigation or criminal proceedings.

Section 31: Consultation with the National Lottery Commission

117. The National Lottery will continue to be regulated by the National Lottery Commission (NLC). This section requires the Commission to consult the NLC about matters in which the NLC is likely to have an interest or where the Secretary of State directs them to do so.

118. The sorts of issues which are likely to be of common concern between the NLC and the Commission are the way in which lotteries are conducted, and in

particular those matters with respect to the conduct of lotteries that are liable to present risks to those taking part. There may be also a mutual interest in whether a particular activity is properly to be described as a lottery or a form of betting.

Section 32: Consultation with Commissioners of Customs and Excise

119. This section requires the Gambling Commission to consult HM Commissioners of Customs and Excise on matters upon which HMCE are likely to have an opinion, or where it is directed to do so by the Secretary of State. This is in addition to the specific requirements for the Commission to consult HMCE concerning its policy statement, codes of practice, and guidance for local authorities.

Schedule 4: The Gambling Commission

120. Schedule 4 provides for the constitution and membership of the Commission established under Part 2 of the Act.

121. The Commission will consist of a chairman and other commissioners. The Secretary of State will appoint all of these. The precise number of Commissioners will be a matter for the discretion of the Secretary of State. The Secretary of State may not appoint a commissioner for a single period of office in excess of five years, or for periods exceeding ten years in total.

122. The chief executive may also hold a position as a commissioner. However, the chief executive may not hold office as chairman. If a person ceases to be chief executive then that also brings to an end that person's appointment as a commissioner.

123. The Commission may also appoint other staff. The terms and conditions of employment of the chief executive and other staff are subject to the consent of the Secretary of State.

124. The Commission may determine its own proceedings, and must publish details of the arrangements it makes. In doing so, the Commission may delegate a function under the Act to: a commissioner, a commissioners' committee, or an employee of the Commission. Such delegation may include any discretionary function, a review function, or the exercise of a regulatory power.

125. *Paragraph 9* authorises the Commission, with the consent of the Secretary of State, to make payments by way of remuneration, allowances, expenses, pensions and gratuities, to commissioners and Commission staff. *Paragraph 10* provides that the Secretary of State may make payments to the Commission to meet such costs as cannot be met out of fees paid to the Commission under the Act. *Paragraph 11* allows the Commission to borrow money, with the approval of the Secretary of State. *Paragraphs 12 to 15* describe the accounting requirements for the Commission, which include a requirement for the Commission's annual statement of accounts to be examined and reported on to Parliament, by the Comptroller and Auditor General.

126. *Paragraph 16* provides that after the end of each financial year the

Commission must send a report of its activities to the Secretary of State. The Secretary of State must lay a copy before Parliament and may arrange for its publication.

Schedule 5: Transfer from Gaming Board to Gambling Commission: supplementary provision

127.   *Paragraphs 1 to 5* of Schedule 5 make a number of technical provisions to achieve the legal transfer of the Gaming Board to the Commission pursuant to section 21. It allows the Commission to step into the shoes of the Board, without prejudicing any action, decision or pending proceedings of the Board. Upon commencement, references to the Board in any legislation or document will be construed as a reference to the Commission. To the extent that the Act has the effect of transferring staff contracts, it is not to affect the protections enjoyed by the staff of the Board under:

- the Transfer of Undertakings (Protection of Employment) Regulations 1981 (TUPE) (SI 1981/1794); or

- any regulations made under section 38 of the Employment Relations Act 1999 (c.26) (which have the effect of replicating TUPE in circumstances where they would not otherwise apply).

128.   In accordance with the Cabinet Office Statement of Practice on Staff Transfers in the Public Sector (January 2000), the Government intend to ensure that those who are currently working for the Gaming Board and who wish to transfer to the Commission are able to do so. To the extent that TUPE does not apply to the transfer of all such staff, provision will be made by regulations under section 38 of the Employment Relations Act 1999 to ensure that in practice its provisions are applied in all cases.

Schedule 6: Exchange of information: persons and bodies

129.   Schedule 6 lists the bodies with which the Commission can exchange information. Under Part 18 of the Act, those bodies listed in Part 1 of Schedule 6 can also pass information to each other.

130.   *Paragraph 1 of Part 3* of Schedule 6 imposes restrictions on information exchanged between the Commission and a Schedule 6 body. In particular, where legislation restricts a Schedule 6 body in the way that it can use information provided to it, the exchange of information provisions in Parts 1 and 18 of the Act cannot override that restriction.

131.   *Paragraph 2 of Part 3* is concerned with information provided to a Schedule 6 body by HM Customs and Excise (HMCE) under this Act. It requires the consent of HMCE to be obtained before that information is passed on to any other body.

PART 3: GENERAL OFFENCES

132. Part 3 contains general offences concerning the provision of facilities for gambling and the use of premises for that purpose. It also contains specific gambling related offences, such as the offences concerned with cheating at gambling and chain gift schemes. In addition to the offences in this Part, the Act contains specific offences concerning particular forms of gambling e.g. making gaming machines available for use (Part 10) or promoting or facilitating a lottery (Part 11) and specific offences relating to gambling involving children and young people (Part 4).

133. All offences under the Act are summary offences, with the exception of the offence of cheating in section 42.

Sections 33 to 35: Provision of facilities for gambling

134. These sections establish the general principle that the provision of facilities for gambling (as defined in section 5) is unlawful unless it is either:

- authorised by an operating licence, or

- covered by a specific exception.

135. The specific exceptions relate to activities which do not require an operating licence under the Act, but which either depend on the issue of a permit or other authorisation, or fall within a category of gambling which may be carried on under the Act without the need for a specific authorisation or permission.

136. There are two further exceptions. The offence does not apply to the provision of facilities for a lottery; and the offence does not apply to making a gaming machine available for use. Specific offences concerning providing facilities in relation to these are contained at Parts 11 and 10 of the Act respectively.

137. *Subsections (4) and (5)* of section 33 provides for the offence to be a summary offence, with a maximum penalty on conviction of imprisonment for 51 weeks for England and Wales (or six months in Scotland), a level 5 fine on the standard scale, or both.

Section 36: Territorial application

138. This section makes provision with respect to the territorial application of the offence of providing facilities for gambling. It provides that, where a person is providing facilities for gambling, it is immaterial whether the facilities are provided wholly or partly by means of remote communication, or inside, outside or partly inside and partly outside the UK. However, where what is involved is remote gambling (defined in section 4 to mean gambling in which those participating do so by means of remote communication), the offence will only apply if at least one piece of remote gambling equipment used in providing the facilities is located in Great

Britain.

139.   This means that, where gambling takes place remotely, the person providing the facilities for gambling will not fall within the scope of the offence if he does not have relevant equipment within Great Britain. This is so even if people within Great Britain can receive the gambling he is providing (e.g. over the internet). On the other hand, where at least one piece of remote gambling equipment is located in Great Britain, a person providing facilities for remote gambling will come within the scope of the offence. Therefore, a person commits the offence if any part of his remote equipment is located in Great Britain and he does not have the required authorisation or is not covered by one of the exceptions. This is so regardless of whether the gambling facilities are provided to people in Great Britain or outside.

140.   *Subsection (4)* defines "remote gambling equipment" for the purposes of the Act:

- *Subsection (4)(a)* captures equipment which stores information e.g. a computer database or server, about a person's participation in gambling. This includes the "game history" of a player, including the player's identity and records of their wins and losses. Equipment used for storage of information for general promotional purposes would not be caught by the definition, unless the information relates to someone's participation in gambling;

- *Subsection (4)(b)* captures equipment used for generating and presenting virtual gambling;

- *Subsection 4(c)* captures equipment used by the person providing the gambling (or on his behalf) for determining the result or the effect of the result of the particular transaction. This covers random number generators used in virtual gaming, or the equipment for calculating whether someone has won or lost a bet on a real event;

- *Subsection 4(d)* captures equipment used to store information relating to a result. This is different to equipment under subsection 4(c) which covers the act of generation of a result, not its subsequent retention.

141.   *Subsection (5)* excludes equipment used by a person who is participating in the remote gambling (i.e. the computer keyboard and screen), provided that the equipment has not been provided by the supplier of the remote gambling.

142.   This section does not restrict the Commission from attaching licence conditions to remote operating licences about the collection and retention of information generally by an operator (under its powers in Part 5). The purpose of this section is to establish whether a remote operator is within the jurisdiction for the purposes of the offence in section 33.

143.   In the case of non-remote gambling (i.e. where remote communication is not used by those participating in the gambling), then the offence will apply if anything

done in the course of the provision of the facilities for gambling is done in Great Britain.

Sections 37 & 38: Use of premises

144.   This section makes it an offence to use premises, or cause or allow premises to be used, for the gambling activities set out in *subsection (1)* unless such use is:

- authorised by an appropriate licence or other permission obtained under the Act; or

- covered by an exception provided in the Act.

145.   The principal authorisations which prevent a person committing an offence under this section are:

- a premises licence under Part 8;

- a temporary use notice under Part 9;

- an occasional use notice under this Part;

- premises used in connection with the provision of facilities for football pools in accordance with an authorisation under this Part;

- a family entertainment centre gaming machine permit under Part 10;

- a club gaming or gaming machine permit, or licensed premises gaming machine permit under Part 12; or

- a prize gaming permit under Part 13.

146.   In addition, there are express exceptions which permit premises to be used for the provision of specified facilities for gambling without the need for a licence or permit, including the provision of gaming machines in premises with an alcohol licence and travelling fairs, and gaming at non-commercial events.

147.   *Subsection (4)* provides an exception for people who are accepting bets on a track, where that track is covered by a premises licence issued under Part 8. In these circumstances the person accepting bets does not himself have to hold a premises licence. This subsection accommodates on-course betting operations, preventing each on-course operator from requiring a separate premises licence, provided the track itself is subject to the appropriate premises licence.

148.   *Subsection (5)* ensures that casino operators can provide betting and (in the case of regional and large casinos) bingo under their casino premises licences without the need for a separate premises licence relating to those facilities.

149.   *Subsection (6)* ensures that no offence is committed where premises are used to provide the facilities listed in subsection (1), provided that those facilities are used only by people who are not on the premises. An example of this is where premises

house a server used for the purposes of remote gambling. *Subsection (6)* also exempts premises which are used only by people acting in the course of business. For example, a telephone call centre set up by a betting operator to accept telephone bets.

150.   This is a summary offence with a maximum penalty on conviction of imprisonment for a term not exceeding 51 weeks for England and Wales (or 6 months in Scotland), a level 5 fine on the standard scale, or both.

151.   Section 38 confers power on the Secretary of State to vary, by order, the gambling activities to which the section 37 offence applies. This includes the power to add or remove a gambling activity to the list provided, or to vary the entry for a gambling activity. The purpose of this provision is, in particular, to ensure that it is possible to bring within the scope of the offence any gambling activities which may be invented in the future, but which are not covered by the list in *subsection (1)*. Where a new gambling activity is added, the Secretary of State may make consequential amendments to Part 8, to provide for an appropriate premises licence, and matters such as machine entitlements.

152.   In particular, an order may have the effect of extending the offence to spread bets or other bets which are subject to regulation under the Financial Services and Markets Act 2000. Spread betting, which is regulated under the 2000 Act, is generally excluded from the scope of this Act (see section 10). The effect of section 38 is to allow the scope of this Act to be extended so that the use of premises to provide facilities for spread betting is also regulated under this Act. In these circumstances, amendments would also be required to Part 8 to enable premises licences to be granted under the Act, authorising premises to be used for the provision of facilities for spread betting.

Section 39: Exception: occasional use notice
153.   This section provides a means for tracks to be authorised for the provision of facilities for betting, where the use (for betting) will be for no more than 8 days a year: the occasional use notice. This notice, when in operation, excepts people on the track from committing the offence of using premises unlawfully for the provision of facilities for gambling. Tracks are defined in the interpretation section in section 353 as a racecourse, dog track or any other premises used or intended for races or other sporting events. The purpose of the section is to ensure that point-to-point racecourses which are used for only a few days a year, and tracks such as golf courses where betting facilities are provided for major competitions, but not otherwise, do not have to obtain a full premises licence in order to avoid the main offence in this Part.

154.   *Subsections (2) to (6)* specify the procedure for serving an occasional use notice. An occasional use notice must be served by an occupier of the track, or a person who is responsible for the administration of races or sporting events on the track. It must be sent to the licensing authority with a copy sent to the police force for the area, and must specify the day on which it is to have effect. An occasional use notice cannot be given for a day in a calendar year if eight occasional use notices have

already been given for days in that year. Therefore, a track that is used more frequently for betting will need a premises licence, or temporary use notice, under Parts 8 or 9.

155.   Any person providing betting facilities pursuant to an occasional use notice will still require the appropriate authorisation to act as a betting operator: in general this will be a betting operating licence, or (in the case of pool betting) authorisation by the holder of a pool betting licence under Part 5.

Section 40: Exception: football pools
156.   Holders of a pool betting operating licence, under section 93, can authorise people who are not their employees to dispense coupons, collect entries and stakes, and pay winnings, on football pools competitions. Collectors can operate, for example, door to door, or from ordinary retail premises such as newsagents.

157.   This section provides an exception for such people from the premises offence in this Part. Collectors can therefore use premises to accept football pools entries, or pay out winnings without committing that offence. *Subsection (2)* gives the Secretary of State power to make regulations, to disapply this concession to particular types of premises.

Section 41: Gambling software
158.   The Act places controls on people who wish to provide facilities for gambling by means of remote communication. This section concerns computer software for gambling that is used in connection with such facilities, but not software designed for use in a gaming machine.

159.   It is an offence under *subsection (1)* to manufacture, supply, install or adapt, in the course of a business, computer software for remote gambling, unless an operating licence is held for such activity. The purpose of this offence is to ensure that people responsible for generating gambling software do so in a regulated environment, to ensure, in particular, fairness for players. While an operating licence for remote gambling covers someone offering gambling, for example by means of the internet, it does not, itself, cover someone who is manufacturing the gambling software that will be used in providing such facilities (i.e. the software supplier to a remote gambling operator). This section covers this latter situation.

160.   The maximum penalty for the offence is a maximum term or imprisonment of 51 weeks in England and Wales (or 6 months in Scotland), and/or a fine up to level 5 on the standard scale.

161.   Computer software for gambling for use in a gaming machine is expressly excluded from this offence (in *subsection (2)(b)*) because the definition of gaming machine in Part 10 already includes such computer software. Someone manufacturing computer software for a gaming machine would therefore be subject to the provisions

(and the offences) contained in Part 10.

162. *Subsection (3)* ensures that a communications service provider, who enables someone to download or send gambling software to another person, is not treated as himself supplying or installing that gambling software. This is an exception for "mere carriers" of the software.

Section 42: Cheating

163. This section creates a criminal offence for cheating at gambling, and repeals the old offence of cheating in section 17 of the Gaming Act 1845 (c.109). The word "cheating" is not defined but has its normal, everyday meaning. The offence is committed by both cheating directly or by doing something for the purpose of assisting or enabling another person to cheat. A person who does something inadvertently which enables another person to cheat, will not, therefore, commit an offence.

164. *Subsection (2)* provides that a person will commit the offence irrespective of whether he actually wins anything as a result of the cheating, or whether the cheating has the effect of improving the cheat's chances of winning. This means that an inept cheat, or one who cheats for another person's benefit, will still commit an offence. *Subsection (3)* provides that, in particular, cheating may include actions that involve actual or attempted deception or interference with the processes involved in the conduct of gambling, or with any other game, race or other event or process to which gambling relates. Events can be either real or virtual. Subsection (3) does not provide an exhaustive definition of cheating. It is made expressly without prejudice to the general meaning of cheating established in subsection (1).

165. *Subsections (4) and (5)* provide for penalties that may be imposed upon conviction of the offence. Unlike other offences created under the Act, this offence is capable of being tried either summarily or on indictment. On summary conviction the penalty is a maximum term or imprisonment of 51 weeks (or 6 months in Scotland), and/or a fine up to level 5 on the standard scale. On conviction on indictment the maximum penalty is imprisonment for a term not exceeding two years, an unlimited fine, or both.

Section 43: Chain-gift schemes

166. This section makes provision for the prohibition of chain-gift schemes. The offence extends to Northern Ireland, as well as England, Scotland and Wales.

167. A chain-gift scheme is an arrangement in which, in order to join, people must pay a joining fee to one or more of the other participants in the scheme. People who take part in the scheme are required or invited to encourage other people to join. A person who participates in the arrangement does so having been encouraged to believe that he will receive back more than his initial joining fee, from the fees paid by other participants. The joining fee must be a payment of money or money's worth, but it

does not include goods or services.

168.   *Subsection (1)* makes it an offence to invite another person to join such a scheme. It is also an offence to knowingly participate in the promotion of the scheme. It will not, however, be an offence for a person merely to join the scheme. People who participate unwittingly in the promotion of a chain gift scheme, such as the host of an internet discussion forum upon which a posting promoting a chain-gift scheme has been made, will not commit an offence, provided they are unaware that the posting promotes a chain-gift scheme. People who knowingly participate in the administration or management of the scheme will also commit an offence.

169.   *Subsection (3)(b)* provides that the offence is committed irrespective of whether the joining fees are paid directly between the participants in the scheme or through a person responsible for managing or administering the scheme. The penalty is a maximum term or imprisonment of 51 weeks in England and Wales (or 6 months in Scotland and Northern Ireland), and/or a fine up to level 5 on the standard scale.

Section 44: Provision of unlawful facilities abroad

170.   This section gives the Secretary of State power to specify countries or places as prohibited territories, with the result that it will be an offence for a person to invite or enable a person in a prohibited territory to participate in remote gambling, where the person making the invitation or enabling the activity does anything in Great Britain or uses any remote gambling equipment in Great Britain so to do.

171.   The Secretary of State's decision whether or not to exercise this power could depend on matters such as: the development of the global gambling market; the laws which other countries establish to permit, constrain or prohibit the use of remote gambling; the practical measures employed by those countries to secure compliance with such laws; and the extent to which it is possible to reach international agreements about the cross-border use of the internet for gambling.

172.   In the event that the Secretary of State makes an order designating countries or places as prohibited territories the order must also prescribe the mode of trial and maximum penalty for the offence.

PART FOUR: PROTECTION OF CHILDREN AND YOUNG PERSONS

173.   Part 4 of the Act creates a number of offences that establish the extent to which children and young people may become involved in gambling, whether in terms of participation in the gambling, entry into gambling premises, or employment in relation to the provision of such facilities.

Section 45: Meaning of child and young person

174.   Under the Act, any person aged less than sixteen years is defined as a child. Any person aged sixteen years or more, but who is not yet eighteen, is defined as a

young person.

Sections 46 & 48: Inviting children and young persons to gamble; participation by young persons in gambling

175.   In broad terms, people aged under eighteen are not to be permitted to gamble. Therefore, it is an offence for a person to invite, cause or permit a person under eighteen to gamble. It is also to be an offence for the young person to gamble (those aged sixteen and seventeen). However, children (those not yet aged sixteen) do not commit an offence if they gamble.

176.   There are some exceptions to the general prohibition on gambling by children and young people. Children and young persons may participate in all forms of private or non-commercial gaming and betting. Young persons may participate in lotteries and pool betting on association football. Children and young persons may use the category of gaming machine with the lowest stakes and prizes (Category D). They may also take part in equal chance prize gaming at certain premises, as provided under Part 13 of the Act.

177.   The offence of inviting a child or young person to gamble is to include advertising and other actions that bring attention to the facilities available for gambling. A person may be liable to commit the offence where his or her name or contact details are included in the information provided to the child or young person, and that person is someone to whom payment may be made or from whom information about the gambling may be obtained. However, in such a case, the person has a defence if he can prove that the information was provided without his consent or authority. A further defence is also available in a case where information is brought to a child's attention (as opposed to being sent to the child). In those circumstances, the person whose contact details appear in the information will have a defence if he can demonstrate that it was brought to the child's attention incidentally to it being brought to the attention of adults.

Sections 47 & 49: Invitation to enter premises; young persons entering premises

178.   Children and young persons may not enter a casino, a betting shop or an adult gaming centre at any time when facilities for gambling are being provided on the premises in reliance on the relevant premises licence. This is subject to the exception that children and young persons may enter the non-gambling area of a regional casino, but they may not enter the gambling area.

179.   Under Part 8, a betting premises licence for a track is subject to the condition that children and young persons are excluded from any area where a Category C gaming machine is available for use or any area where facilities for betting are provided. However, the latter restriction does not apply in the case of a dog-race track or a horse-race course on any day on which racing takes place (see section 182).

180.   Children are equally not permitted to enter areas of family entertainment

centres where Category C gaming machines are available for use.

181.   Any person who invites a child or young person to enter these premises, or the parts of the premises described above, commits an offence. Where a young person enters these areas, he too commits an offence.

182.   As a consequence of these provisions, a person of any age may enter bingo premises, the betting areas of a horse racecourse or a greyhound track on days on which races are being run, or the non-gambling area of a regional casino. A person of any age may also enter any area of a family entertainment centre where no Category C gaming machines are provided at that place. This does not mean that they can necessarily partake in any gambling on the premises, see sections 46 and 48.

Section 50: Provision of facilities for gambling
183.   A young person commits an offence if he provides facilities for gambling, except in connection with private or non-commercial gaming and betting, lotteries, football pools and prize gaming at a travelling fair.

Sections 51 to 55: Employment offences
184.   It is an offence to employ children and young persons to provide facilities for gambling, except in the case of private or non-commercial gaming and betting and in relation to prize gaming at a travelling fair. There is a further exception in the case of lotteries and football pool betting. In those cases, the offence only extends to the employment of children and not young persons. The National Lottery is excluded from this provision. Regulations made under the National Lottery etc. Act   1993 already prohibit the sale of National Lottery tickets to those under 16.

185.   Restrictions are imposed on the ways in which children and young people can be employed to work on premises where facilities for gambling are provided, even if they are not engaged to perform any gambling activities themselves. This is to ensure that children and young people are not afforded undesirable exposure to gambling.

186.   It is an offence to employ children to work in premises at any time when facilities for the playing of bingo are being provided on the premises. It is also an offence to employ children at a club or institute at any time when facilities for gambling are being provided pursuant to a permit (section 53).

187.   In relation to any premises where gaming machines of any category are situated, then any child or young person employed may not perform any function that involves the gaming machine. Therefore, for example, a child may be employed in a family entertainment centre to undertake non-gambling activities, although he may not operate or handle the machine or pay customers prizes in the event that the machine has insufficient money in it (and he may not enter the area where the Category C machines are located) (section 54).

188.   Generally children and young persons are not allowed to be employed in any

capacity in casinos, betting premises and adult gaming centres. This is subject to an exception in the case of regional casinos where children and young persons can be employed in non-gambling areas. It is possible, however, for children and young persons to be employed in adult only gambling premises (small and large casinos, the gambling area of regional casinos, betting offices and adult gaming centres) when no facilities for gambling are being provided. Therefore, for example, a sixteen-year-old apprentice joiner may undertake improvement works on the structure of a bar in a casino when it is closed (section 55).

189.   There is also an effective prohibition on children and young persons being employed in the betting areas of certain tracks and the adult-only areas of family entertainment centres. This follows the provisions referred to above which generally prohibit children and young persons from being able to enter such areas (sections 47 and 49).

Section 56: Invitation to participate in lottery
190.   This section makes it an offence to invite, cause or permit a child to take part in a lottery, for example, by selling him a ticket. However, this offence does not apply to two types of lottery allowed under the Act, that is, private lotteries and incidental non-commercial lotteries (see Schedule 11, Parts 1 and 2). This means that the section does not, for example, prevent the sale to children of tickets in events such as the tombola at a school or church fete. The National Lottery is also excluded from this provision.

191.   The Act does not criminalise the purchase by a child of a ticket in any form of lottery.

Section 57: Invitation to participate in football pools
192.   Young people are to be permitted to participate in football pools, and it is, therefore, permissible for the operators of football pools to provide information to young persons, or to direct advertisements to young persons. However, children may not participate in football pools and this section makes it an offence to invite, cause or permit a child to do so.

Section 58: Return of stake
193.   Under Part 5, all operating licences for gambling are subject to a condition requiring licence holders to return any money paid to them by children or young persons, where the person concerned is not permitted to participate in the gambling activity (section 83). It also requires the licence holder to withhold any winnings that would otherwise be payable. This section makes it an offence for a licence holder to fail to do so.

Section 59: Age limit for category D machines
194.   The Act does not set a minimum age limit for the use of Category D gaming machines. This section gives the Secretary of State power by order to establish one, by creating an offence of inviting, causing or permitting a child or young person

below a specified age to use a Category D gaming machine.

195.   Before making such an order, the Secretary of State is required to consult the Commission, people who appear to the Secretary of State to represent the interests of gambling businesses and people who have knowledge about problem gambling. An order need not apply to all types of Category D machine, which means that an age limit can be imposed on particular types of Category D machine.   Therefore, if the evidence dictates that only certain types of machine require an age limit (as a result of harm), the section ensures that only those machines will be covered by the limit.

Section 60: Temporary use notice
196.   Temporary use notices issued under Part 9 may authorise gambling at premises that do not have a premises licence. The same applies in the case of premises subject to an occasional use notice. For the purposes of this Part, the relevant areas of such premises are to be regarded as being subject to the equivalent premises licence. Therefore, where a temporary use notice authorises gaming in one part of a hotel, a young person working in the hotel may not enter that area during the time that the notice has effect.

Section 61: Meaning of employment
197.   For the purposes of this Part, employment is to be regarded as having a wide meaning. For example, as well as direct employees of the licence holder, people engaged temporarily through an employment agency are equally to be regarded as employees of the licence holder.

198.   Any offence committed under this Part will be treated as a continuing offence which means that a new offence will be committed on each day that the employment continues. This increases the level of penalty that will be available in sentencing.

Section 62: Penalty
199.   Offences under this Part are to be punishable on conviction by a maximum term of imprisonment of up to 51 weeks in England and Wales (or 6 months in Scotland), or a fine not exceeding level 5 on the standard scale, or both. Where it is young person who is convicted, imprisonment is not to be available and any fine imposed may not exceed level 3 on the standard scale.

Section 63: Reasonable belief about a person's age
200.   Where a person is charged with an offence under this Part of doing anything in relation to a child or young person it is to be a defence for the person to prove that he took all reasonable steps to determine the relevant person's age and he reasonably believed that the person was not a child or a young person.

Section 64: Use of children in enforcement operations
201.   This section will enable children and young persons to be used in test purchasing operations for the purpose of assessing whether the provisions in this Part, prohibiting under-age gambling, are being complied with. For example, a constable,

enforcement officer or authorised person will not commit an offence under section 46 if, in the course of their duty, they invite a child or young person to gamble. Equally, a young person will not commit an offence under section 48 if he gambles at the request of a constable, enforcement officer or authorised officer who is acting in the course of his functions.

PART 5: OPERATING LICENCES

202.   Operating licences are one of the principal forms of authorisation under the Act for the lawful provision of facilities for gambling. A person holding an operating licence, and providing facilities within the terms and conditions of that licence, will not commit the offence of unlawful provision of facilities for gambling under Part 3.

203.   The sections in this Part describe the licensing regime to be administered by the Commission for granting operating licences. Matters covered include the principles to be applied by the Commission in considering applications for operating licences, powers for conditions to be attached to licences, and the review procedures once licences have been granted.

204.   There are different kinds of operating licences for the various forms of gambling facilities e.g. to operate a casino, to provide facilities for betting, or to act as a betting intermediary. An operating licence for each kind of activity can authorise the provision of facilities on premises generally ("non-remote provision") or for the provision of those facilities by means of remote communication ("remote provision"). However, it is not possible to combine a licence for both remote and non-remote provision (but one person can be granted both a remote licence for betting and a non-remote licence for betting).

205.   An operating licence for non-remote provision gives a <u>general</u> authorisation for the operator to provide gambling facilities on premises. However, before being able to use any <u>particular</u> premises, the holder of an operating licence will also need an authorisation under the Act to use such premises for gambling. The principal form of such permission is a premises licence granted under Part 8 of the Act, although there are other forms of permission e.g. an occasional use notice (section 39) or a temporary use notice (Part 9).

206.   In addition to authorising the provision of facilities for gambling, operating licences can be obtained to authorise:

- the manufacture, supply, installation, adaptation, maintenance and repair of gaming machines; and

- the manufacture, supply, installation and adaptation of gambling computer software.

207.   Part 1 of the Act defines "betting", "gaming" and "lottery", and a number of

related concepts. Part 18 of the Act contains further interpretation provisions relevant to Part 5.

Section 65: Nature of licence

208.   There are ten different kinds of operating licence:

    a) a casino operating licence;
    b) a bingo operating licence;
    c) a general betting operating licence;
    d) a pool betting operating licence;
    e) a betting intermediary operating licence;
    f) a gaming machine general operating licence for an adult gaming centre;
    g) a gaming machine general operating licence for a family entertainment centre;
    h) a gaming machine technical licence;
    i) a gambling software operating licence; and
    j) a lottery operating licence.

209.   *Subsection (1)* empowers the Commission to issue these operating licences. *Subsection (4)* allows the Secretary of State, through secondary legislation, to amend this list so as to add, vary or delete a class of operating licence.

Section 66: Form of licence

210.   A licence must specify the person to whom it is issued; how long it has effect; and any condition attached to the licence by the Commission (*subsection (1)*). The Secretary of State may set out in regulations further details of what information a licence must contain, and the form in which it is to be issued (*subsection (2)*).

Section 67: Remote gambling

211.   Facilities for gambling can be provided remotely (i.e. by technology which means the player is not in the same place as the person offering the facilities), or non-remotely (i.e. face to face on premises). This section defines a "remote operating licence" as an operating licence which authorises someone to provide remote gambling, and requires all licences to state whether they are a remote operating licence or a non-remote operating licence. An operating licence cannot be both.

212.   The effect of this section is that for each of the ten kinds of operating licence listed in section 65, there are two basic types: a remote operating licence which authorises, for example, the provision of particular facilities by means of the internet; and a non-remote licence, which authorises the same facilities to be provided from premises. It will not be possible for one operating licence to combine authorisations for providing both remote and non-remote facilities for gambling. One person can hold both types of licence, but he will need to be granted each separately.

213.   Further provisions on the conditions which can be attached to a remote licence

allow the Commission to limit the particular forms of remote communication by which gambling is offered under a remote licence. Therefore, a remote licence does not automatically confer an entitlement to use all forms of remote communication e.g. television, radio and the internet. Instead, conditions can limit provision to one, or any combination of the different forms of remote communication defined in Part 1.

Section 68: Combined licence

214.   While there is a distinction between remote and non-remote operating licences, meaning that they cannot be combined in one licence, the Commission can issue operating licences which cover more than one of the ten kinds of licence, provided they are all either remote, or non-remote.

215.   The starting point, *in subsection (1)*, is that one operating licence can authorise a combination of the different kinds of activities that make up the ten kinds of operating licence. However, this is subject to certain rules and limitations.

216.   Under *subsection (3)* a casino operating licence also authorises the provision of facilities for betting on the outcome of a virtual game, race, competition or other event or process (to the extent that this is not restricted or excluded by a condition imposed by the Commission), and the provision of equal chance gaming, other than bingo. This means that a casino operator does not need to obtain a betting operating licence if he wishes to offer this form of betting, and can automatically offer equal chance gaming, other than bingo. If he does wish to offer bingo, he will need to obtain a bingo operating licence as well. Under rules in Part 8 of the Act, a small non-remote casino cannot offer bingo from its premises.

217.   Under *subsection (4)*, a betting operating licence authorises the provision of facilities for betting on the outcome of a virtual game, race, competition or other event or process (other than a game of chance), but only to the extent that this is not restricted or excluded by a condition imposed by the Commission. This gives the Commission power to regulate virtual betting if the need arises.

218.   Neither subsections (3) or (4) are authorisations for virtual gambling by machine. Machine gambling is regulated by Parts 8 and 10 of the Act. These subsections concern over-the-counter, person to person, betting on virtual events, or remote gambling where no gaming machine is involved.

219.   There are two types of operating licence specifically designed for authorising the provision of gaming machines: the gaming machine general operating licence for adult gaming centres and the gaming machine general operating licence for family entertainment centres. These specifically authorise the licence holder to make gaming machines available for use. However, under *subsection (5)* certain other types of operating licence also bring with them a general entitlement to make gaming machines available for use:

- a non-remote casino operating licence;

- a non-remote bingo operating licence;

- a non-remote general betting operating licence; and

- a non-remote pool betting operating licence.

220.   Apart from these four types of operating licence (and the two general gaming machine operating licences) no other operating licences may authorise the making available of gaming machines. Therefore, no remote operating licence confers a right to make gaming machines available for use.

221.   Moreover, the fact that certain operating licences provide this authorisation, does not entitle the holder of the licence to use any number or category of gaming machines, on any particular premises. The purpose of subsection (5) is to provide a generic authority for the operator to make gaming machines available for use, in the same way as a casino operating licence gives authority to provide facilities to operate a casino (in the general sense). The provisions of Parts 8 (premises licences) and 10 (gaming machines) control the precise locations where gaming machines may be used, and an operator must comply with the requirements of these Parts to make a gaming machine available for use lawfully.

Section 69: Application

222.   This section sets out who may apply for an operating licence and the type of information that must accompany an application. Applications are to be made to the Commission and such other people as the Secretary of State directs. The application, in particular, must contain details of the gambling activities that the operator wishes to provide (e.g. which of the ten types of licence he wishes to obtain, and whether remotely or non-remotely), and state whether the applicant has been convicted of a relevant offence (as defined in the interpretation section for this Part).

223.   An application fee is payable, which may vary for different types of licence (i.e. different kinds of gambling activity) or different circumstances (*subsections (2)(g) and (5)*). Such fees will be prescribed by the Secretary of State in regulations. It is anticipated that fees will vary across sectors to reflect the Commission's differing costs of regulation.

Section 70: Consideration of applications: general principles

224.   This section sets out the general principles which the Commission will apply in determining applications, and particular matters which they may take into account. The detail of how the Commission will consider applications, and, for example, what evidence it will seek, will be set out in the statement of licensing policy that the Commission is required to produce under Part 2 of the Act.

225.   The purpose of this section is to outline the principles which will govern the Commission's decision-making in relation to the consideration of applications. The two main matters are: to have regard to the licensing objectives, and to have regard to the applicant's suitability, including his integrity, competence, and financial

circumstances. The assessment may also cover the suitability of equipment to be used in connection with the proposed activities.

226. The Commission's assessment may cover not just the applicant, but also people who are connected to the applicant because they are likely to exercise a function in connection with, or have an interest in, the gambling activities.

227. *Subsection (3)* makes specific provision for those cases where the application is for a non-remote casino operating licence. In such cases, the Commission must have regard to the applicant's commitment to protecting vulnerable people from being harmed or exploited by gambling, and to making assistance available to people who may be affected by problem gambling. This requirement reflects the particular risks presented by casinos in relation to problem gambling.

228. There may be circumstances where the Commission will wish to assume that a class of applicant will automatically fulfil the requirement of integrity for the purpose of assessing suitability. In these circumstances the Commission's statement may make a determination to this effect. For example, the Commission could decide that local authorities, seeking a lottery operating licence, do not need to supply evidence of integrity as part of the application process.

229. The Commission can also deem particular equipment or gaming machines to be suitable, in accordance with standards or tests that it has established, or asked others to establish for it. This is designed to aid both the Commission and applicants in making the application process as efficient as possible.

Section 71: Consideration of application: criminal record
230. One of the licensing objectives is to keep gambling crime free. This section provides that the Commission may refuse an application for an operating licence if the applicant has a conviction for a relevant offence. This is without prejudice to the suitability of the applicant generally, but permits the Commission to reject an application by reason of the conviction for the relevant offence, should it consider this appropriate. "Relevant offence" is defined in the interpretation section for this Part.

Section 72: Consideration of application: demand
231. Under the Betting, Gaming and Lotteries Act 1963 and the Gaming Act 1968, one of the considerations for the grant of a permit or licence was whether there was unmet demand for the specified gambling facilities in the particular area to which an application related. This section revokes this principle, as unmet demand is not a relevant criterion, under the Act, for determining whether or not to grant an operating licence. This section also abolishes the "permitted areas" for casinos which were established under the Gaming Act 1968. Similar provisions are contained in Part 8, in relation to the consideration of premises licences. The necessary repeals for these various matters are set out in Schedule 17.

Section 73: Procedure

232.   This section sets out the powers of the Commission to require information from an applicant, and to have regard to information provided by other people when considering an application. In particular, the Commission may require the production of an enhanced criminal record certificate under the Police Act 1997 (c.50). This applies to the applicant or people relevant to the application.

233.   The licensing policy statement produced by the Commission under Part 2 must specify the procedures to be operated by the Commission, including the Commission's practice with regard to delegating functions, holding hearings, and requiring evidence. Schedule 4 also makes provisions with regard to the general proceedings of the Commission.

Section 74: Determination of application

234.   This section provides the range of determinations the Commission can make having considered an application and the actions consequent upon a determination, including a requirement to give reasons where an application is rejected.

Sections 75 to 78: Licence Conditions

235.   There are three types of licence condition that may be attached to operating licences under the Act: general conditions and individual conditions, both of which are attached by the Commission; and conditions imposed by the Secretary of State.

236.   Sections 75 and 76 concern general conditions, which are conditions the Commission may specify for an operating licence or a class of operating licence, and which have general application. So, for example, the Commission could specify a general condition that applied to all general betting operating licences, that the rules of the bet must be on display to customers (whether on premises, or over the internet). This condition would apply to everyone holding a general betting operating licence.

237.   Section 76 sets out the procedures which the Commission must follow in specifying general conditions. These include holding general consultations (with some mandatory consultees) on the terms of the condition, and publishing conditions. In addition, the Commission must notify licensees in advance of a proposed imposition, modification or revocation of a general condition, giving three months notice, unless the matter is urgent. This ensures that licensees have adequate notice of general conditions and changes that may be made to them over time.

238.   Additionally, the Commission has power, under section 77 to impose specific conditions on individual operating licences. These conditions are not subject to any publication or general consultation requirements, in contrast with general conditions. Rather, these conditions will address particular matters concerning an individual operator and its activities, where the Commission considers it appropriate. So, for example, the Commission could attach an individual condition on a particular casino operating licence that not more than five casino premises can be operated under it, due to the financial strength of the operator. Every operating licence issued must specify

any individual conditions attached to it under this section.

239.   Alongside the powers of the Commission to attach conditions to operating licences, the Secretary of State may make regulations which provide for a specific condition to be attached to a class of operating licence, under section 78.

Section 79: Scope of powers to attach conditions
240.   This section gives specific examples of the matters to which general, individual or Secretary of State conditions may relate. The section does not limit the breadth of the matters with which these three types of condition can deal. Instead, this section helps provide some understanding of the matters which conditions may cover.

241.   A condition may:

- limit or restrict the nature or extent of the gambling facilities provided, or control the circumstances in which they are carried on;

- make provision about the facilities that may be provided, the manner in which the facilities are provided or the number of people employed in providing facilities;

- make provision about the financial resources available to the licensee, including the maintenance of reserves in respect of potential liabilities;

- where it is a remote operating licence, may restrict the methods of remote communication that may be used;

- make provision about the advertising or description of facilities for gambling (which could include the name given to a gambling product);

- make provision about assistance to people who are or may be affected by problem gambling; and

- require the operator to identify or record the identity of users of his facilities.

Section 80: Requirement for personal licence
242.   Part 6 of the Act provides the licensing system for personal licences. This section sets out the relationship between an operating licence and the need for an operator to use people holding personal licences to provide certain functions and facilities for gambling.

243.   When the Commission considers an application for an operating licence, it will consider what offices or functions in the organisation should be performed by a personal licence holder, and attach conditions to the licence specifying what the requirements for personal licences are to be. These conditions could be set by general or individual condition, or the Secretary of State may set generic conditions by regulations to apply to classes of operating licence.

244.   There will be one mandatory condition on every operating licence, which is

that every operating licence must specify at least one management office which is to be occupied by a person who holds a personal licence (*subsection (1)*). This will be set as a general or individual condition, not a Secretary of State condition. Beyond this one mandatory personal licence, the Commission may identify any additional number of posts in an operator's organisation which must be filled by a personal licence holder (*subsections (2) to (4)*). Such conditions will always relate to either a management office or an operational function.

245.   Management office (*subsection (5)*) means:

- A director of a company;

- A partner;

- An officer in an unincorporated association; and

- Any position which (by reason of the terms of the appointment) carries responsibility for:

    - the conduct of a person who performs an operational function; or
    - facilitating or ensuring compliance with the terms of the operating licence.

246.   Operational function *(subsection (6))* means:

- any function that enables the person to influence the outcome of gambling;

- receiving or paying money in connection with the gambling; or

- specified activities in relation to the manufacture and supply of gaming machines.

247.   The Secretary of State has the power to amend these definitions through secondary legislation (*subsection (8)*).

248.   These broad definitions will enable the Commission to consider the particular circumstances of each operator (irrespective of the job titles the operator may use) and identify those functions and offices within an organisation that will require a person to hold a personal licence when carrying them out.   This section is not intended to require everyone performing any management office or operational function (as described above) to hold a personal licence. The Commission will decide what the appropriate licensing requirements are to be, either on an individual basis, or, where it is able to do so, according to classes of operating licence.

249.   If an operator does not use a person holding an appropriate personal licence to perform an office or function identified by the Commission, it will breach a condition of its operating licence.

250.   While this section provides the mechanism for operating licences to contain conditions about matters to be undertaken by a personal licence holder, it does not

cover the process for obtaining a personal licence. That is set out at Part 6 of the Act.

251.   *Subsection (9)* contains an exemption from the requirements of this section for clubs or miners' welfare institutes holding a bingo operating licence. Part 12 requires clubs or miners' welfare institutes which provide facilities for bingo that exceed a specified threshold in terms of stakes or prizes in any week, to obtain a bingo operating licence. Games played below this threshold are authorised by other provisions in Part 12. Officers of these associations are not required to hold personal licences in relation to their additional bingo operating licence, and this subsection exempts them accordingly.

Section 81: Credit and inducements
252.   This section concerns restrictions on the offering of credit and inducements by operating licence holders. *Subsection (1)* provides that a condition may be attached by the Commission to an operating licence relating to:

- the giving of credit in relation to the licensed gambling activities;

- making offers or inducements designed to induce participation in the licensed gambling activities; or

- being party to arrangements for inducing, permitting or assisting person to gamble.

253.   In addition to this general condition-making power, s*ubsection (2)* provides that holders of non-remote casino or bingo licences may not themselves give any form of credit to people using their facilities. Nor may they arrange, permit or knowingly facilitate credit in connection with their gambling facilities. This means that credit cards cannot be used to pay for gambling offered by casino or bingo operators. A similar restriction is placed upon the relevant premises licences in Part 8, and Part 10 prevents credit cards being used to pay for gaming machines.

254.   Subsection (3) allows cash-withdrawal machines accepting credit cards to be used by casino or bingo operators, provided that:

- the nature and location of the machines complies with any relevant licence conditions; and

- the provider of the machine and the gambling operator are unconnected, and no payment is made or received in connection with the machine.

255.   *Subsection 4* defines "credit" to include any form of financial accommodation and the acceptance of payment of a fee, charge, or stake in anything other than cash, cheque or debit card payment is considered credit.

Section 82: Compliance with code of practice
256.   This section makes it a condition of all operating licences that the holder must comply with any code of practice relating to social responsibility which is relevant

to them. Codes of practice issued by the Commission under Part 2 are not of themselves automatically binding on operators, but are part of the overall scheme of regulation. However, this section provides that social responsibility provisions in any code are incorporated as conditions to an operating licence.

Section 83: Return of stakes to children

257.   The Act contains a range of provisions designed to prevent children and young people from gambling. Under this section a condition is imposed on all operating licences which requires operators to take certain steps in the event that they become aware that a child or young person has used their facilities to gamble. A child is a person under 16, and a young person a person under 18.

258.   If an operator becomes aware that a child or young person has used his gambling facilities, then the operator must return any money paid by the child or young person as soon as practicable, and must not pay out any winnings (although if winnings have been paid out before the operator is aware of the claimant's age, he may not demand repayment).

259.   This section does not apply to the use of the lowest stake gaming machine (a Category D machine) or equal chance gaming at a licensed Family Entertainment Centre (which can be played pursuant to authorisations under Part 13). The section only applies to children (and not a young person) when the gambling activity concerned is football pools or a lottery. The condition imposed by this section cannot be overridden by any contract or other agreement.

Section 84: Premises

260.   It is the role of licensing authorities to licence specific premises upon which facilities for gambling may be provided in Great Britain. These matters are regulated by Part 8 of the Act. Therefore, an operating licence cannot be subject to a condition which specifies particular premises upon which gambling activities must or must not be carried on. However, conditions may be attached to operating licences which deal with the number of sets of premises on which the licensed activities may be carried on (e.g. a maximum of 100 betting shops) or the number of people for whom facilities may be provided on any premises where the licensed activities are carried on.

261.   An operating licence is not limited to authorising the provision of facilities in one place. The fact that an operating licence is a "casino" operating licence or an operating licence for an "adult gaming centre" does not mean this only authorises the provision of one such facility. An operating licence gives a generic entitlement, to be used alongside any number of premises licences, subject to any conditions imposed under subsection (1) of this section.

Section 85: Equipment

262.   In issuing an operating licence, the Commission may attach a condition about the amount or specification of equipment to be used in the licensed gambling activities. Such equipment may include computers or devices for playing casino

games, but does not include a gaming machine. This ties in with the powers of the Commission to consider the suitability of equipment when considering an application for a licence.

263.   The section contains a specific provision for equipment used for playing bingo. Under *subsection (2)(a)* a condition cannot be attached to a licence about the number of pieces of equipment used for playing bingo. This means that equipment such as "mechanised cash bingo equipment", used under the Gaming Act 1968 regime, cannot be subject to control about its numbers. It can be subject to licence conditions about its specification under *subsection (2)(b)*, and such specification will enable this equipment to fall outside the definition of gaming machine in Part 10.

264.   Similarly, the Commission can use subsection (2)(b) to specify equipment for playing bingo in adult gaming centres or licensed family entertainment centres, (bingo played pursuant to the prize gaming entitlements in Part 13). Where it does so, such equipment will not constitute a gaming machine.

Section 86: Gaming machines

265.   While certain operating licences confer general permissions to use gaming machines, under section 68, the permission to use gaming machines on particular premises is contained in Parts 8 and 10 of the Act. This means that the Commission should not attach conditions to operating licences concerning numbers or categories of gaming machines which an operator is entitled to use. Therefore, *subsection (1)* prevents operating licences having conditions attached to them about:

- the number or categories of gaming machine that may be made available for use in accordance with an operating licence; or

- anything that contradicts regulations concerning the use of gaming machines, made by the Secretary of State under Part 10.

266.   This does not mean that the Commission cannot regulate the manufacture and supply of machines. Section 96 makes express provision for the Commission to set standards for the gaming machine technical operating licence.

267.   *Subsection (2)* provides a mechanism for the Commission to require operators to stop using machines that have been illegally manufactured, supplied, or handled. The Commission may notify an operator that a machine is not covered by an appropriate gaming machine technical operating licence, or does not comply with Commission standards. After such notification, the Commission may place a condition on the relevant operating licence requiring the operator to stop making the machine available for use. Failure to do so will amount to breach of the licence.

Section 87: Membership

268.   Under the Gaming Act 1968 it is a requirement that gaming licences under Part II of that Act can only be held by casinos or bingo halls that operate as a members' club. That rule is abolished by this Act, and as a result, this section

provides that neither the Commission nor the Secretary of State can impose a condition on an operating licence requiring facilities to be provided on the basis of a club or on any other membership basis. However, nothing in this section or the rest of the Act prevents organisations from operating as a members' club if they so wish.

Section 88: Information

269.   This section permits the Commission or the Secretary of State to impose licence conditions requiring operators to pass information to the Commission or to such other people as may be specified. The purpose of this power is to promote information exchange between the Commission, operators and, for example, sporting regulators. The type of information which could be covered includes information concerning cheating or breach of sporting rules. Licence conditions could also be used to supplement the voiding of bets powers in Part 17. Voluntary codes are already in place in parts of the gambling industry to allow such information exchange. This section allows a uniform approach for different sectors to be established, as appropriate.

Section 89: Remote operating licence

270.   This section sets out particular rules applying to a remote operating licence.

271.   It is a presumption of a remote operating licence that remote gambling equipment used by the operator in providing facilities for gambling must be located in Great Britain. This is set out in *subsection (1)*. Part 3 contains the definition of remote gambling equipment.

272.   *Subsection (2)* empowers the Commission to depart from this general presumption, in certain circumstances. The Commission may allow an operator to site particular pieces of specified remote gambling equipment off-shore, provided the Commission is satisfied that to do so is consistent with the licensing objectives in section 1. For example, the power could be used in relation to equipment facilitating player to player games which can involve individuals in different jurisdictions being pooled by operators. The matter is one of discretion, for the Commission.

273.   Without prejudice to its other condition-making powers, the Commission may establish, or authorise others to establish on its behalf, standards in respect of systems and processes used for remote gambling. These standards will be relevant to the consideration of applications for remote operating licences, made under section 69. The Commission can enforce these standards through licence conditions, including the testing of the operator's systems, on application and from time to time.

Section 90: Casino operating licence

274.   Part 1 provides a definition of casino, and gives the Secretary of State powers to define categories of casino. Under *subsection (1)* the Commission or the Secretary of State can impose conditions on any casino operating licence which restricts the type of casino game that can be made available. Under the Gaming Act 1968 these restrictions were imposed by secondary legislation. Under the Act the Commission

has the power to achieve this by licence condition, or the Secretary of State may do so by regulations.

275.   *Subsection (2)* provides that the Commission may specify rules for casino games or any equal chance game played in a casino. Again, this power replaces the position under the Gaming Act where these matters were prescribed in secondary legislation.

Section 91: Bingo operating licence

276.   The Secretary of State may use her regulation making to attach conditions to bingo operating licences on the matters specified in *subsection (1)*. This includes power to limit the amount of stakes or participation fees or value of prizes; or requiring a specified proportion of stakes to be paid out by way or prizes, or imposing requirements specific to bingo games that are played on more than one set of premises. *Subsection (2)* then lists matters about which conditions cannot be made in relation to bingo operating licences. This means that the Commission has no power to set conditions on these matters, and, to the extent that it is not expressly permitted by subsection (1), nor does the Secretary of State.

277.   The introduction of remote operating licences, together with the Secretary of State's power to impose requirements that are specific to games played on more than one set of premises, at *subsection (1)(e)*, replace the statutory provisions relating to "multiple" and "linked" bingo that are repealed by this Act. Remote operating licences will be required by those wishing to provide bingo by means of remote communication, even where the bingo is played partly on licensed bingo premises. The fees for these licences will be commensurate with the regulatory costs for the particular activities concerned.

278.   *Subsection (2)(f)* prevents a condition being attached to a bingo operating licence which prohibits or limits the roll-over of prizes between bingo games. Neither the Secretary of State, nor the Commission can attach a condition relating to the roll-over of prizes.

279.   In setting participation fees under subsection (1), different types of fee may be set, as amplified by section 344. For example, fees for admission to the premises can be distinguished from a fee to participate in a particular game. Fees can also be apportioned between gambling and non-gambling purposes.

Section 92: General betting operating licence

280.   A general betting operating licence will be required by anyone wishing to accept or make bets by way of business (this includes negotiation of bets). If someone wishes to provide facilities merely for other people to accept and make bets, then the relevant operating licence will be a betting intermediary operating licence, not a general betting operating licence, as the latter is relevant only for people who are themselves making or accepting bets in the course of a business. See also sections

353(2)(a), 296(3) and 302.

281.   This licence replaces the bookmaker's permit under section 2 of, and Schedule 1, to the Betting, Gaming and Lotteries Act 1963.

282.   *Subsection (1)* sets out who is empowered to accept bets under the terms of a general betting operating licence: this will be the licence holder, an employee of the licence holder and any other holder of a general betting operating licence. No other person may accept or make bets under the authorisation of a general betting operating licence.

283.   *Subsection (2)* makes it clear that a general betting operating licence contains an implied term permitting the making of bets via postal services. This prevents any question of the need for a remote licence arising in relation to bets made by post.

Section 93: Pool betting operating licence
284.   Where an operator is making or accepting pool bets (as defined in section 12), then the appropriate operating licence will be a pool betting operating licence. This type of licence may cover any form of pool betting, but conditions may limit the particular pool betting activities an operator may provide. For example, a pool betting operating licence may specify that the operator may only operate pool betting in relation to football pools.

285.   This licence replaces the system for registration of pools promoters under section 4 of, and Schedule 2 to, the Betting, Gaming and Lotteries Act 1963. It is also the form of authorisation that will be required by operators of pool betting on dog-tracks, previously authorised by section 4(1)(b) of the 1963 Act. Part 8 of this Act contains separate provisions governing the use of dog-track premises for pool betting. Horserace pool betting is dealt with in the next section.

286.   As with the general betting operating licence, there are restrictions on who is permitted to accept pool bets under the licence. The restrictions are the same as those for the general betting operating licence, except that pool betting operators will also be allowed to authorise agents to accept bets on their behalf in certain circumstances. Those circumstances are:

- where the agent is on a track in reliance on an occasional use notice and is accepting bets in relation to a horse-race or a dog race on that track. In these circumstances the agent must be an adult and be authorised in writing to accept bets on behalf of the licensee (*subsection (2)*); or

- where the pool betting operating licence permits the operator to provide football pools and the operator has given written authority to an adult or young person to receive entries or payments on football pools on his behalf ("authorised collector") (*subsections (3) to (6)*). In these circumstances the authorised collector may provide coupons, receive entries and payments, and pay winnings, pursuant to the   operating licence. Conditions may also be imposed on the operating licence specific to the authorised collectors.

287.   Under *subsection (9)* the Secretary of State may change, by order, the types of event on a track (subject to an occasional use notice) for which an agent may be authorised to take pool bets under subsection (2), and may add sports to the matters for which agents can be authorised under subsection (3), in addition to football pools.

288.   *Subsection (7)* makes it clear that a pool betting operating licence contains an implied term permitting the making of pool bets via postal services. This prevents any question of the need for a remote licence.

Section 94: Horse-race pool betting operating licence

289.   Where a pool betting licence authorises the provision of horserace pool betting, then the operating licence may specify that this section has effect. The intention is that this section will be needed in circumstances where only one licence for horserace pool betting has effect in Great Britain.

290.   Under *subsection (2)*, the holder of a pool betting licence, who is licensed to conduct horserace pool betting, may authorise in writing any person to provide facilities for horserace pool betting, and this authorisation may include terms as to payment. This means that, for example, such an authority may be used by a person to accept pool bets on horse races on premises with a betting premises licence, or pursuant to an occasional use notice. This authorisation may also be made the subject of specific conditions on the operating licence (*subsection (5)*). *Subsection (6)* makes it clear that a pool betting operating licence contains an implied term permitting the making of pool bets via postal services.

291.   The Secretary of State has the power to repeal this section if circumstances dictate that it is no longer needed i.e. if there are no longer exclusive arrangements for horserace pool betting in Great Britain. In such circumstances, the pool betting operating licence would become the only kind of licence relevant to pool betting in Great Britain, and would also cover horserace pool betting. Section 358(4) to (6) makes specific provision concerning commencement of this Act, and transitional powers relating to the Horserace Betting Olympic Lottery Act 2004 (c.25).

Section 95: Betting on the National Lottery

292.   This section replaces provisions in the Betting, Gaming and Lotteries Act 1963 which caused a bookmaker to lose his licence if he took bets on the outcome of the National Lottery (Schedule 1, paragraph 18A). Under this section, all types of operating licences permitting betting are subject to a mandatory condition that no betting takes place on the outcome of the National Lottery.

Section 96: Gaming machine technical operating licence

293.   Without prejudice to other condition-making powers, the Commission may establish, or authorise others to establish on its behalf, standards in respect of systems and processes used for the manufacture, supply, installation, adaptation, maintenance

or repair of a gaming machine, or software for use in a gaming machine (*subsection (1)*). These standards must be consistent with the rules concerning gaming machines contained in Part 10 (*subsection (2)*).

294.　These standards may cover technical matters about the functioning of the machines. Under *subsection (3)* they may also cover matters such as the nature of the gambling involved, the way in which the results are presented or determined, and the nature of the information displayed on the machine. This is intended to be used, in particular, to provide standards which discourage repetitive play and protect children.

295.　The Commission can enforce these standards through licence conditions, including the testing of the operator's systems on application, and from time to time.

Section 97: Gambling software: operating licence: standards
296.　This section permits the Commission to set standards for gambling software supply and manufacture for use in remote gambling. Similar powers are set out in sections 89 and 96 for remote gambling and gaming machines respectively. The section describes the powers the Commission has, including authorising individuals to test software, or a random sample of software and requiring licensees to make software available for testing.

Section 98: Lottery operating licences
297.　This section provides for the Commission to issue licences for the operation of lotteries. Lotteries which form part of the National Lottery (which are not covered by this Act), or that are classed as "exempt" lotteries under Schedule 11, will not require a licence under these provisions.

298.　A lottery operating licence may only be issued to the following:

- non-commercial societies;
- local authorities; and
- external lottery managers.

299.　Section 18 of the Act contains a definition of "non-commercial society". A non-commercial society, which wishes to hold lotteries, will only require an operating licence under this section if the proceeds of the lotteries they promote exceed the thresholds set out in Part 4 of Schedule 11 to the Act. Below these thresholds, the lottery will be classified as a "small society lottery", and will be exempt from the requirement to obtain a licence (although they will require registration with a local authority).

300.　The types of local authority which may promote a lottery are broadly defined, and include parish councils in England, and community councils in Wales (*subsection (7)*).

301. *Subsection (2)* allows the Commission flexibility in terms of the scope of operating licences. A licence may authorise promotion generally, or specific promotion activities. It may authorise promotion of lotteries generally, or only in connection with lotteries of certain types or in certain circumstances.

302. A licence may authorise a person to act as an external lottery manager, to provide lottery management services on behalf of local authorities, and on behalf of non-commercial societies, whether licensed or exempt. The Commission has the power to include a condition on a lottery operating licence that all of the arrangements for the lottery are to be made by an external lottery manager. If the Commission does so, it will not be required to form an opinion about the suitability of the local authority or non-commercial society in terms of integrity, competence or financial and other circumstances (under section 70(2)), when considering their application for a licence. Their assessment will be of the lottery manager only. The Commission may similarly assume the integrity of particular classes of applicant, and, for example, could do so where a local authority is making the application (see section 70(7)).

303. *Subsections (4) and (5)* ensure that it will not be possible to prohibit the delivery of lottery tickets by post in relation to these lotteries, either by regulations made by the Secretary of State, or by conditions made by the Commission. *Subsection (6)* specifically empowers the Commission to attach conditions to the licence concerning rollovers, that is the carry over of prizes from one lottery to another, as defined in Part 11.

Section 99: Mandatory conditions of lottery operating licence
304. This section provides that the Commission must attach certain conditions to lottery operating licences issued to non-commercial societies and local authorities, for the purpose of achieving the requirements set out in the section. The Commission is not restricted to these conditions, and may attach conditions which are similar, but more onerous, than those specified here.

305. Various conditions must be attached to licences which set money or percentage limits in relation to proceeds and prizes. At least 20% of the proceeds of any lottery promoted under the licence must go to good causes. In the case of a non-commercial society, this means that a minimum of 20% of the proceeds must be used for the purposes for which the society is conducted. In the case of a local authority, 20% of the proceeds must be put towards a purpose for which it has the power to incur expenditure. Under all lottery operating licences, the proceeds of any single lottery must be limited, and the proceeds of all lotteries in one year are restricted to an overall upper limit. There is also an upper limit on the size of a prize in a licensed lottery. These limits are set out in *subsections (2) to (4)*.

306. Conditions must be attached to the licence prescribing certain requirements in relation to tickets. In particular, the information specified in *subsections (5) and (6)* must be included on the ticket. One ticket may provide entry to a number of lotteries, provided the information contained on it is sufficient that the dates of the draws in

those lotteries are able to be determined. A ticket need not be a paper document, but if it is in electronic form, it must be capable of being printed out or electronically stored (*subsection (7)*). This will permit, for example, entry to a lottery over the internet. No additional payment apart from the ticket price may be required for entry into the lottery (*subsection (8)*).

307.   The Secretary of State has power to vary, by order, the money amounts and percentages set out in this section (*subsection (10)*).

Section 100: Annual fee
308.   The holder of an operating licence must pay a fee to the Commission for the licence to have effect ("the first annual fee"), and, thereafter must pay an annual fee before each anniversary of the issue of the licence. These annual fees acts as renewal fees in the sense that failure to pay them can lead to revocation of the licence. These fees are different to the application fee required when making an application for a licence. The Secretary of State will use regulations to set the fees and the period within which the first annual fee must be paid. Different fees may be set for different kinds of operating licences and different circumstances.

Section 101: Change of circumstance
309.   If an operator has a change of circumstance after an operating licence is issued he may be required, by regulations (under this section) or by conditions attached to his licence, to inform the Commission of the change of circumstance. There is a fee to be paid by for the operator. The Commission must then amend the licence as appropriate to reflect the change in circumstances.

310.   This section sets out the regulation making power of the Secretary of State, and provides that a licence holder commits an offence if he fails, without reasonable excuse, to comply with a requirement to inform the Commission of a change of circumstance. The maximum penalty for the offence is a fine not exceeding level 2 on the standard scale. The Commission may also suspend or revoke an operating licence if the holder fails to comply with regulations under this section.

Sections 102 & 103: Change of corporate control
311.   If the holder of an operating licence is a company limited by shares, a mechanism is needed to allow the Commission to approve a change of control of that company (i.e. following sale, transfer, allotment or issue of shares). These sections provide that mechanism.

312.   This mechanism applies to any kind of operating licence, but the Secretary of State may make regulations exempting specified kinds of operating licence from these requirements.

313.   This section uses the definitions set out in the Financial Services and Markets Act 2000. It provides that if a person becomes a "controller" of a company which holds an operating licence ("the company"), then the company must surrender the

licence to the Commission, or apply to the Commission for approval for the licence to continue to have effect.

314. If the company wishes to apply for approval for the licence to continue to have effect (which will attract a fee to be set by the Secretary of State), then the Commission may require information about the change of control and the new controller. The Commission may give approval if it is satisfied that that it would have granted the operating licence at the time of the original application, had the new controller been the controller of the company at the time. If it is not so satisfied, then the Commission must revoke the operating licence. A company has five weeks from the date when the new controller takes over in which to surrender its licence, or apply for a continuation, otherwise the Commission will revoke the licence (unless the Commission chooses to extend this period, which it may do, even after the 5 weeks has expired, provide the licence has not already been revoked).

315. In requiring information in relation to a change of control, the Commission is required to have regard to normal commercial practices concerning confidentiality.

316. These sections apply to the merger or division of companies, but where this is the cause of a change of controller, the Secretary of State may set reduced fees for applications in these circumstances.

Section 104: Application to vary licence
317. Holders of operating licences may, for their own commercial reasons, wish to vary the gambling facilities that they provide, whether that is to cease carrying out an activity, or to start a new activity. Equally, they may wish to vary an individual condition that has been attached to their licence. In such circumstances, the holder of an operating licence will need to apply to the Commission to vary the terms of the licence.

318. This section permits holders to apply for a variation of an operating licence, and applies the provisions of Part 5, modified as appropriate, to the variation process. Regulations by the Secretary of State will provide the relevant procedures.

319. An application for variation cannot be used to transfer an operating licence to another person. Operating licences are non-transferable.

Section 105: Amendment
320. This section provides that the Commission may require the holder of an operating licence to submit the licence to the Commission for amendment in a number of circumstances where it requires changes to be made to it.

321. A licence holder has 14 days to comply with a requirement to send his licence to the Commission in response to a request, and commits an offence if he fails to do so without reasonable excuse. The maximum penalty is a fine not exceeding level 2 on the standard scale. The Commission also has power to suspend or revoke a licence

if the holder fails to comply with the requirements set out here.

Section 106: Register of operating licences

322.   To allow the public to find out whether a person providing gambling facilities holds the necessary permission, licence or permit, the Act contains a series of requirements for various registers to be maintained. This section requires the Commission to maintain a register of operating licences and to make it available to the public. A fee may be payable to gain access to the register, but the fee must not exceed the reasonable cost of providing the service.

Sections 107 & 108: Copy of licence and production of licence

323.   These sections allow the Commission:

- to issue to a licence holder a copy of the licence in the event that it has been lost, stolen or damaged; and

- (together with the police) to require the holder of an operating licence to produce it within a specified period. The licensee will be committing an offence if he fails without reasonable excuse to comply with this requirement. The maximum penalty is a fine not exceeding level 2 on the standard scale.

Section 109: Conviction

324.   One of the licensing objectives in the Act is to prevent gambling from being a source of crime or disorder, being associated with crime or disorder or being used to support crime. This section requires holders of operating licences to take certain steps in the event that they are convicted of a criminal offence in Great Britain or abroad.

325.   Where the holder of an operating licence is convicted of an offence in Great Britain, or of a relevant offence by a court outside Great Britain, he must inform the Commission as soon as reasonably practical. This ensures that the Commission has the necessary information it needs to regulate licence holders, and could, if it wished, commence a review of the licence.

326.   If the holder of an operating licence is convicted of a relevant offence before a court in Great Britain he must inform the court immediately that he holds an operating licence. This is so that the court can consider whether it should exercise its powers to order forfeiture of the operating licence as part of the sentence it imposes for the offence.

327.   A list of offences which are "relevant offences" is set out at Schedule 7. These are offences under British law (the jurisdictions of England and Wales, and Scotland). An offence under the law of another country is a relevant offence if it is similar in nature to an offence listed in Schedule 7. This ensures that a person's suitability to hold a licence is considered in relation to any criminal conviction for a serious offence, not just those in Great Britain (see section 126 for the definition of "relevant offence").

Sections 110 & 111: Duration

328.   As a general rule, operating licences will be of indefinite duration, subject to rules about lapse, forfeiture and the Commission's regulatory powers. However, the Commission has power to determine that operating licences, or a particular class of operating licence, should be given a particular duration. Such a determination will be made and promulgated as part of the Commission's licensing policy statement under Part 2.

329.   Where the Commission determines a particular duration under section 111, this will apply to existing and future licences. However, for existing licences the duration will begin from the date of publication of the determination rather than the date the licence was granted.

Section 112: Renewal of licence

330.   This section provides that where the Commission has decided that operating licences are to have a fixed duration under section 111, procedures for the renewal of licences can be put in place.

Sections 113 & 114: Surrender and Lapse

331.   A licence ceases to have effect if it is surrendered to the Commission. This provides a voluntary procedure for a licence holder to give up his licence if he so wishes.

332.   A licence will lapse, and is not transferable, if the licence holder:

- Dies;

- In the opinion of the Commission becomes incapable of carrying out the licensed activities (from which there is a right of appeal); or

- Becomes bankrupt or goes into liquidation.

Section 115: Forfeiture

333.   This section provides courts with the power to order forfeiture of an operating licence where it is sentencing the holder of a licence on conviction for a relevant offence, as defined in section 126. This allows the courts to take appropriate steps to bring a licence to an end, without the Commission needing to take separate regulatory action.

Section 116: Review

334.   Section 110 provides that operating licences are granted for an indefinite period. However, the Commission has power to introduce time limits for licences if it believes there is a regulatory need to do so. Therefore, the general position is that licences will not need to be renewed at any point. Section 116 gives the Commission the power to review, over time, the performance of licence holders and the operation of licence conditions.

335. First, under *subsection (1)* the Commission may review matters relating to a class of operating licence i.e. not an individual licence, but a type of licence. For example, the Commission could review the operation of all gaming machine general operating licences. The purpose will be to review the manner in which licensees, as a whole, carry on licensed activities, and particularly, how licensees comply with the conditions attached to the class of operating licence. The purpose of this type of review could be to consider whether any changes to general conditions on licences are needed.

336. Secondly, under *subsection (2)*, the Commission has power to review any matter relating to an individual operating licence on any of three grounds:

- If the Commission suspects that conditions of an operating licence are being breached;

- If the Commission believes that the licence holder or any person connected with the gambling activities, has been convicted of a relevant offence in Great Britain or abroad; or

- If the Commission for any reason:

  - suspects that the licence holder may be unsuitable to perform the licensed activities; or
  - thinks that a review would be appropriate.

337. The section makes it clear that a review can be carried out even if there is no suspicion or belief about the licence holder's activities. This ensures that a licence could be reviewed solely on the grounds, for example, that it had been held for a long period of time, and that the Commission considered a review prudent.

338. In the event that the Commission decides to carry out a review of an individual licence there are procedural requirements to ensure that the licence holder can take part in the review (*subsections (4) and (5)*).

Sections 117 to 121: Regulatory powers
339. The Commission has a range of powers available to it, exercisable after a review, or in circumstances where a licence holder has failed to comply with other requirements specified in Part 5 of the Act (e.g. to pay the annual fee). These sections outline these powers, and the procedural steps the Commission must take before exercising them.

340. The Commission can:

- give the licensee a warning;

- add, remove or vary a condition to the licence;

- make, amend or remove an exclusion;

- suspend or revoke the licence; or

- impose a financial penalty.

341. Suspension powers are available to the Commission at the outset of, and during, a review. Therefore, if the Commission considers a matter sufficiently serious, it can require the operator to suspend all or part of his activities pending the outcome of the review. The Commission also has powers to suspend a licence following a review.

342. Where the Commission concludes that a licence holder has breached the conditions of his licence, it may impose a financial penalty on the licence holder. The Commission must take a number of procedural steps before it can impose such a penalty, which include providing the licence holder with reasons for the proposed penalty, and time in which to make representations to the Commission. The Commission is subject to a time limit for imposing a penalty of two years following the date of the breach, or the date the Commission becomes aware of the breach, whichever is later.

343. To ensure that licence holders are aware of the way in which the Commission intends to use its power to impose financial penalties, the Commission must prepare and publish a statement of the principles it will apply in exercising these powers. In particular, the Commission must, in considering the imposition of a penalty, have regard for the seriousness of the breach of condition, whether the licensee knew or ought to have known of the breach and the nature of the licensee (including his financial resources). Before preparing or revising such a statement the Commission must consult the Secretary of State, the Lord Chancellor and other people as the Commission thinks appropriate.

344. All the regulatory powers available to the Commission under these sections are subject to full rights of appeal for those affected by them, under Part 7, to the Gambling Appeals Tribunal.

Section 122: Information
345. To assist the Commission to carry out its functions, this section sets out obligations on licence holders to comply with requests for information. These cannot be "fishing exercises" by the Commission, but must concern questions of whether the licence holder has breached his licence conditions, or is unsuitable to carry on gambling activities. Non-compliance without reasonable excuse is an offence that will attract a fine not exceeding level 2 on the standard scale.

Section 123: Levy
346. This section provides the Secretary of State with reserve powers to impose an annual financial levy on the holders of all operating licences. The power cannot be exercised in relation to particular classes of operating licence. If introduced, the levy will apply to all classes of operating licence. The levy would be paid to the Commission, and treated as if it were part of the annual fee. This means that a

licence would be revocable if the levy was not paid.

347.   The money raised by a levy would be used for alleviating problem gambling. Thus, the Commission could spend it on purposes or projects related to gambling addiction or other forms of harm or exploitation associated with gambling. The Treasury and the Secretary of State must consent to the Commission's expenditure of the levy. Such projects need not be undertaken by the Commission itself, but the Commission could fund others (including other public sector bodies) who are undertaking projects connected with problem gambling.

348.   The section sets out the matters relating to the levy which must be set out in the regulations. A number of alternative methods for calculating the levy are listed, but none are mandatory. Depending on the method of calculation chosen, different levies could be charged to different operators. Before making these regulations imposing a levy, the Secretary of State must consult the Commission.

349.   Provision is made, under Schedule 3 to the Act, for the National Lottery to be made subject to levy requirements also. A levy in these circumstances could not be imposed until the powers under this section had been exercised.

Section 125: Relevant offence: disapplication of rehabilitation
350.   This section identifies certain circumstances when section 4 of the Rehabilitation of Offenders Act 1974 (c.53) will not apply. This means that the Commission will be able to look at spent convictions in some cases. Where a person has a conviction for a relevant offence (defined in section 126) then the Commission will be able to consider a spent conviction for the offence when a person applies for an operating licence.

Section 126: Interpretation
351.   This section provides definitions for terms used throughout Part 5, including "relevant offence".

Schedule 7: Relevant offences
352.   This Schedule lists the British offences which are "relevant offences" for the purposes of the Act (in England, Wales and Scotland). Under section 126 a relevant offence can also be a foreign offence which is equivalent to an offence listed in Schedule 7.

353.   Under Part 5 of the Act, the Commission has power to take relevant offences into account when considering applications for operating and personal licences. Where an offence is a relevant offence, the Commission may consider such offences during the application process, even though they are spent within the terms of the Rehabilitation of Offenders Act 1974.

354.   When sentencing a person convicted of a relevant offence, a court in Great Britain may order forfeiture of an operating or personal licence held by that person as

part of the sentence. Where the licence held is a personal licence, the court may also disqualify the person from holding a personal licence for a period of up to 10 years, when it is sentencing for a relevant offence.

355. While the Commission may take account of a domestic, unspent conviction for any offence when considering an application for a licence under Part 5 of the Act, it is only those offences listed in this Schedule that attract the particular provisions regarding spent convictions, foreign offences, forfeiture and disqualification.

PART 6 – PERSONAL LICENCES

356. This Part of the Act deals with personal licences, which certain individuals working in the gambling industry will be required to hold. The Commission will grant these licences, which are of indefinite duration. This regime is also relevant to operating licence holders, who will be required to use personnel who hold a personal licence. Unless the operator is a small-scale operator, the Commission is obliged to use its condition making powers to ensure that, for each operating licence, at least one person occupies a specified management office and holds a personal licence authorising them to perform the functions of the office.

357. Part 6 operates on the basis that many of the provisions contained in Part 5 on operating licences are also relevant to personal licences. So, in relation to many of the procedural requirements which the Commission will need to undertake for the personal licensing regime, the sections in Part 5 are deemed to apply to personal licences under Part 6. Powers are taken for the Secretary of State to make necessary modifications to the Part 5 procedures. This approach has been adopted to avoid repetition of large amounts of material in both Parts 5 and 6. Where particular matters need a self-standing provision for personal licences, Part 6 provides accordingly.

Section 127: Nature of personal licence
358. A personal licence will authorise the holder to perform a specified management office or specified operational function, in connection with either the provision of facilities for gambling or a person who provides such facilities. The definitions of "management office" and "operational function" are set out in section 80.

359. By attaching conditions to operating licences under Part 5, the Commission will identify posts which must be held by a personal licence holder. These fall into the two groups of management offices and operational functions. Therefore, personal licences may need to be held by those directly providing the facilities for gambling, such as a croupier, or those who perform certain functions in a gambling operation but do not actually themselves provide the facilities, such as a compliance officer. Not everyone who works in the gambling industry will need a personal licence. It will be the task of the Commission, in granting operating licences, to determine which posts within any organisation need to be held by someone with a personal licence, and

operators must employ people accordingly.

Section 128: Application of provisions of Part 5

360.   The personal licensing system under Part 6 is not intended to be a free-standing regime in its own right, but instead sits alongside the regime for operating licences in Part 5. This section specifies that Part 6 is to be read as incorporating the features of the operating licence system, except where:

- it is modified by Part 6, or as necessary; or

- it is amended by regulations made by the Secretary of State.

361.   As a result, the basic procedures for application for, determination of, and review of licences will be the same for both operating and personal licences, except where this Part (or the natural context) demands otherwise. Personal licences may be subject to general or specific conditions imposed by the Commission, or conditions imposed by the Secretary of State in regulations.

362.   Personal licences are different to the ten types of operating licence specified in section 65(2).

Section 129: Exemption for small scale operators

363.   Part 5 requires that anyone holding an operating licence must have at least one person in a management office holding a personal licence. However, this section exempts small-scale operators from this requirement. This is because, in small operations, the operating licence will achieve the same purpose as a personal licence. For example, an independent on-course betting operator, employing only one or two people is likely to be the sort of operator who will be excused from holding a personal licence under this section.

364.   The Secretary of State will define the meaning of "small scale operator" in particular by reference to the size and value of the business, and the number of employees (*subsection (2)*). *Subsection (4)* requires an operator, who benefits from this exemption, to produce his operating licence, as if it were a personal licence. Section 134 sets out the requirements for producing a personal licence.

Section 130: Application

365.   The application procedures set by the Commission for personal licences will mirror those set out in Part 5, with suitable modifications. In particular, the licensing objectives, and the applicant's suitability (including integrity and competence) will be taken into account by the Commission in deciding whether to grant a licence. This section makes it clear that the Commission can require the applicant's employer or intended employer to take part in the application process for a personal licence (*subsections (1) and (2)*). However, a person does not have to be employed in order to apply for a personal licence (*subsection (4)*). A person may acquire a licence prior to

seeking employment in order, for example, to improve his chances of finding work.

Sections 131 & 135: Duration and Review

366.   Subject to surrender, lapse, forfeiture or revocation, all personal licences will be of unlimited duration. The Commission does not have the power to introduce limited durations for personal licences, as it can for operating licences under Part 5.

367.   The review procedures for individual licences contained in section 116 will apply to personal licences, with any appropriate modification. However, the power to review classes of licence is not available for personal licences.

Section 132: Fees

368.   Personal licences will be subject to an application fee. Under this section the Secretary of State also has power to specify periodic fees to be paid by a personal licence holder to the Commission to maintain his licence. Unlike operating licence maintenance fees, these will not necessarily be annual fees. Instead, the Secretary of State may set the amount and the period for which the fees must be paid. Non-payment can lead to revocation of a personal licence. The maintenance fees will be used by the Commission to cover the costs of regulation.

Section 133: Multiple licences

369.   An individual will not be allowed to hold more than one personal licence, but a personal licence can cover a number of management or operational functions. This allows one individual to conduct a number of functions relying upon one licence.

Section 134: Production of licence

370.   This section gives police constables and Commission enforcement officers the power to require a personal licensee to produce his licence within a specified period. If the individual is carrying on a licensed activity, or is on licensed premises, then the licence must be produced immediately. This means that a personal licence holder will be required to keep the licence on his person when at work. This is in contrast to the operating licence holder, who, unless they are a "small scale operator" can only be required to produce the operating licence within a specified period. Failing to comply with these requirements will be an offence, attracting a fine not exceeding level 2 upon conviction.

Section 136: Disqualification

371.   In addition to being able to order forfeiture of a personal licence as part of the sentence for a relevant offence, this section allows a court to order that the person be disqualified from holding a personal licence for a period of up to ten years. This can be instead of, or in addition to, an order for forfeiture. Relevant offences are defined under section 126 of the Act.

Sections 137 & 138: Notification requirements

372.   Where the Commission suspends or revokes a personal licence, or a court orders forfeiture or disqualification, the operating licence holder is entitled to be

notified by the Commission of what has happened to the personal licence. Equally, where an operating licence holder is aware that a personal licensee has been convicted of a relevant offence, he must inform the Commission of the fact.

Section 139: Breach of personal licence condition

373. This section makes it an offence for the holder of a personal licence to breach a condition of his licence, when acting in the course of (or in connection with) an activity authorised by an operating licence, which itself requires the personal licence to be held. The holder of the operating licence may also commit an offence, on the same set of facts, under Part 5, but this section provides that the individual personal licence holder can be proceeded against for the offence, irrespective of what steps are taken against the operator. The penalty for the personal licence holder is a maximum period of imprisonment in England or Wales of 51 weeks, and in Scotland of 6 months, and/or a fine not exceeding level 5.

PART 7: OPERATING AND PERSONAL LICENCES: APPEALS

374. Part 7 provides for the formation and operation of an independent tribunal to deal with gambling matters. It will deal with appeals against decisions taken by the Commission in respect of operating and personal licences (Parts 5 and 6 of the Act), as well as appeals in relation to a decision by the Commission to void a bet under Part 17.

Section 140: The Gambling Appeals Tribunal

375. This section provides for the establishment of the Gambling Appeals Tribunal. The requirements for the foundation and operation of the tribunal are set out in Schedule 8 to the Act. The purpose of the Tribunal is to hear appeals against the decisions of the Commission. The mechanism for appeals against the decisions of licensing authorities are set out in those Parts and Schedules of the Act which deal with the functions of such authorities e.g. Part 8 on premises licences and Part 9 on temporary use notices.

Section 141: Appeal to Tribunal

376. Rights of appeal are available to people affected by the decisions of the Commission. This section sets out the particular circumstances under which holders of, and applicants for, operating and personal licences will have a right of appeal against decisions of the Commission:

- A person who has applied for grant of an operating or personal licence, (or, when relevant, an existing licence holder who has applied for renewal of their licence), will have the right of appeal against the Commission's decision.

- Where the Commission attach an individual condition to an operating or personal licence, the holder of the licence will have the right of appeal against the decision.

- An operating licence holder that is a company limited by shares, which has applied for the operating licence to continue to have effect when a new controller takes over, can appeal against the Commission's determination.

- The holder of an operating or personal licence who has applied to the Commission for variation of the licence by adding, amending or removing an authorised activity; amending another detail of the licence; or adding, amending or removing an individual condition attached to the licence, may appeal against the Commission's decision.

- The holder of an operating or personal licence can appeal against a decision by the Commission that they are incapable of carrying on their licensed activities by reason of mental or physical incapacity.

- The holder of an operating or personal licence can appeal against the Commission's use of its regulatory powers in connection with a review: that means that an appeal can be made against the issue of a warning to the licence holder; the variation or removal of a condition or exclusion, or attachment of a new condition or exclusion to the licence; suspension or revocation of the licence; or imposition of a financial penalty.

Section 142: Timing

377.   This section provides for a time limit within which an appeal must be commenced. An appeal must be made within one month of the date of decision or action that is to be appealed against. However, the Tribunal has discretion to permit an appeal to be started after this period.

Section 143: Appeal from Tribunal

378.   This section provides that parties to an appeal before the Tribunal may appeal the Tribunal's decision to either the High Court, or, in Scotland, the Court of Session. The right only extends to appeals based on a point of law, and appeals may only be brought with the permission of the Tribunal or, if this is denied, the relevant appeal court. A higher court to which an appeal is brought under this section can affirm or quash the Tribunal's decision, or remit the matter back to the Tribunal for a re-determination. There is no power for the higher court to make a fresh determination based on the facts of the case.

Section 144: Powers of Tribunal

379.   This section provides for the Tribunal's powers following an appeal. It allows the Tribunal to either uphold or overturn all of, or part of, the Commission's decision. The Tribunal can also substitute a decision or action taken by the Commission for another. In so doing, it is limited to taking only decisions or actions of a kind which the Commission is empowered to take. For example; if the Commission recommended that a financial penalty be imposed, the Tribunal could rule that a more appropriate decision would be to revoke the licence, or to issue a warning. But the Tribunal cannot order something which the Commission could not have ordered in the first place.

380.   The Tribunal can also add to the Commission's decisions, i.e. it could uphold a decision to impose a financial penalty, and add that the licence should also be revoked. This section also allows for the Tribunal to refer a matter back to the Commission for further consideration, following which there will again be the right to appeal to the Tribunal under this Part from the new decision made by the Commission.

381.   The Tribunal can also re-instate a lapsed or revoked licence following a successful appeal.

382.   When determining an appeal, the Tribunal can take into account evidence that was not previously available to the Commission, and it must ensure that it considers any relevant code of practice issued by the Commission.

Section 145: Stay pending appeal

383.   This section provides that a decision or action of the Commission, in relation to an operating or personal licence, will not have effect until either the period for bringing an appeal has expired, or if an appeal is in progress, until the appeal has been finally determined or abandoned. For example, if a financial penalty is imposed, and this is appealed against, the penalty cannot be enforced until the Tribunal decides, following that appeal, whether to uphold the decision to impose the penalty.

384.   However, the Commission has the discretion to disapply this stay in a particular case if, for example, it considers that it is necessary that a particular licence is revoked or suspended with immediate effect. In such circumstances, the bringing of an appeal will not prevent the Commission's decision having effect, pending the outcome of the appeal. This power is provided so that the Commission can ensure fairness to players, protection of children and the vulnerable, and the prevention of crime (the licensing objectives).

Section 146: Rules

385.   This section gives the Lord Chancellor the power to make secondary legislation in relation to the regulation of appeals to the Tribunal, and the procedure of proceedings before the Tribunal. In particular, these rules may specify who can be a party to proceedings, including, specifically, for the purposes of an appeal against a decision of the Tribunal. *Paragraph 14* of Schedule 8 gives a non-exhaustive list of matters about which rules can be made. It includes:

* the manner and time in which appeals are instituted;
* determination of ongoing issues during the course of proceedings and other ancillary matters;
* issuing directions to parties;
* disclosure;
* joining the Commission to proceedings;

- suspension of Commission decisions;

- giving evidence and production of documents;

- administration of oaths to witnesses;

- public admission to proceedings;

- representation of parties;

- withdrawal of proceedings;

- recording and declaration of decisions;

- award of costs or expenses;

- variation or revocation of Tribunal decisions.

386.   Rules made under this section may make it an offence not to comply with certain requirements.

Section 147: Fees
387.   This section enables the Lord Chancellor, through regulations, to set the level of fees to be paid by a person when bringing an appeal to the Tribunal. Different fees for different types of case or circumstance may be charged, and the Tribunal may waive a fee where it deems it appropriate. The Lord Chancellor must consult the Secretary of State before exercising this power.

Section 148: Legal Assistance
388.   This section enables the Lord Chancellor, through regulations, to establish a legal assistance scheme to provide financial assistance to appellants who might otherwise be unable to instigate an appeal to the Tribunal. Regulations may specify the kinds of assistance that may be provided and the classes of person by whom assistance may be provided. They may also include provision about applications to the Tribunal for assistance, including a requirement to provide information. The Lord Chancellor may state the criteria to be used by the Tribunal in determining eligibility for legal assistance, and may make provision for an applicant to appeal against a decision to refuse assistance. This section does not apply to Scotland, where different powers for affording legal assistance are available.

Section 149: Enforcement of Costs Orders
389.   This section enables an award of costs made by the Tribunal to be enforced as though it was an order of the county court. The judgement creditor must apply to the county court for the district in which the debtor resides and payment may be enforced in accordance with Part V of the County Courts Act 1984. This includes the power to call in the bailiffs if necessary.

Schedule 8: Gambling Appeals Tribunal
390.   This schedule sets out the provisions for the establishment, constitution, and procedure of the Gambling Appeals Tribunal, and should be read in conjunction with

this Part.

Paragraphs 1 and 2: President, deputy and members

391.   The Lord Chancellor will appoint a President and has the authority to appoint other members to the Tribunal. Only those with appropriate legal qualifications can be appointed. The Lord Chancellor can also appoint one or more members of the Tribunal to be its deputy President, who will act when the President is absent, and will undertake other duties delegated by the President.

Paragraph 3: Tenure

392.   The duration of post of the President or other members of the Tribunal is dependent upon the terms and conditions of appointment. Resignation must be in writing to the Lord Chancellor. The Lord Chancellor has the power to dismiss Tribunal members, including the President and deputy President, for misbehaviour, or if they are unable or unwilling to undertake their duties. The retirement provisions contained in the Pensions and Retirement Act 1993 will apply to all tribunal members.

Paragraph 4: Staff

393.   The Lord Chancellor can appoint staff for the Tribunal.

Paragraphs 5 to 8: Money

394.   The Lord Chancellor has the power to pay Tribunal members, including the President and deputy President, and staff. He also has the power to pay other expenses of the Tribunal. Money received by way of appeal fees is to be paid into the Consolidated Fund. The President of the Gambling Appeals Tribunal qualifies for a pension under the Judicial Pensions and Retirement Act 1993.

Paragraph 9 to 11: Sittings

395.   The Tribunal President will direct when and where the Tribunal sits and will decide which members are to be present at each sitting. This is in line with general arrangements made by the Lord Chancellor. At each sitting of the Tribunal, the President or a Tribunal member must be present. It will also be possible for the President to sit with two Tribunal members, for example, in a case which is considered to be particularly complex. The arrangements may provide that in some cases, a three member Tribunal may be obliged to continue sitting with only one or two members. In such a case, if sitting with just one other member, the arrangements may include provision for the President to have a casting vote.

396.   The President will determine the constitution of the Tribunal and the times and places at which it will sit, in accordance with the general arrangements made by the Lord Chancellor. The Lord Chancellor must consult the President before making general arrangements. Arrangements made by the Lord Chancellor will be published.

Paragraphs 12 to 14: Procedure

397.   Tribunal decisions are to be taken by a majority vote. The President is empowered to give directions about the practice and procedure of the Tribunal, as

long as these do not conflict with the rules made by the Lord Chancellor.

Paragraph 15: Council on Tribunals

398.   The Gambling Appeals Tribunal will be subject to the scrutiny of the Council on Tribunals, which is responsible for the supervision, constitution and working of Tribunals and Inquiries in England, Scotland and Wales, under the Tribunals and Inquiries Act 1992 (c.53).

Paragraph 16: Disqualification

399.   This paragraph disqualifies any member of the Tribunal from being a member of the House of Commons and prevents the President of the Tribunal from practising as a solicitor or barrister whilst in post.

PART 8: PREMISES LICENCES

400.   Part 8 of the Act describes the new regime for the licensing of premises where facilities for gambling may be provided. Premises licences are the third main category of licence (operating and personal licences being the other two) that will be issued under the Act. Premises licences will be granted by licensing authorities (as defined in section 2), not the Commission.

401.   In England and Wales licensing authority functions are conferred on local authorities, and in Scotland upon licensing boards, as defined in Part 1 of the Act. Scottish Ministers will exercise a number of powers under this Part, prescribing procedures and fees for the premises licensing system in Scotland.

402.   Premises licences can authorise the provision of facilities on:

- Casino premises;
- Bingo premises;
- Betting premises, including tracks and premises used by betting intermediaries;
- Adult Gaming Centres (for Category B,C and D machines); and
- Family Entertainment Centres (for Category C and D machines)

403.   However, premises licences are not the only form of authorisation for the use of premises for providing gambling facilities. Under the Act, permission may also be obtained through:

- Occasional use notices or football pools authorisations under Part 3 of the Act;
- Temporary use notices under Part 9 of the Act;
- Permits for family entertainment centres (Category D machines only) under Part 10 of the Act;

- Authorisations for alcohol licensed premises; clubs and miners' welfare institutes and travelling fairs, all under Part 12 of the Act;

- Permissions for prize gaming under Part 13 of the Act; and

- Authorisations for private and non-commercial gaming and betting under Part 14 of the Act.

404. Applicants for premises licences are required to hold a relevant operating licence before being granted a premises licence under this Part, except in the case of tracks, where an operating licence need not be held in all cases. This is to enable trackside betting operators (also known as on-course bookmakers) with operating licences to benefit from the track premises licence held by the occupier of the track. Pool-betting on a track, by the track occupier, will require a pool betting operating licence to be held. The definition of a "track" is contained in section 353.

405. Premises licences, unlike operating licences, are transferable between occupiers (who hold operating licences), on application to the licensing authority. Conditions on premises licences can be set by the licensing authority, and by the Secretary of State, or Scottish Ministers. Licensing authorities have powers to review licences, with associated regulatory powers. A provisional statement may be obtained from a licensing authority, in advance of a premises licence, where premises are to be constructed or altered, or where someone has yet to acquire the right to occupy premises.

406. Part 8 provides appeals mechanisms for people affected by the decisions of licensing authorities.

407. Part 18 contains provisions requiring all licensing authorities to set three-year licensing policies in respect of all of their functions under the Act, including premises licences. It also provides prosecution powers for licensing authorities in relation to their licensing functions.

408. Part 10 contains provisions concerning gaming machines, and the categorisation of machines by the Secretary of State. A reference to a Commission code of practice in this Part is a reference to a statutory code of practice issued under Part 2 of the Act.

Section 150: Nature of licence
409. This section describes, in *subsection (1)*, the premises licences that may be issued by a licensing authority. They are:

- A licence for the operation of a casino;

- A licence for the provision of facilities for playing bingo;

- A licence for making Category B gaming machines available for use (an adult gaming centre);

- A licence for making Category C gaming machines available for use (a family entertainment centre); and

- A licence for the provision of facilities for betting, including betting intermediary facilities

410. Under Part 1 of the Act, the Secretary of State will make regulations defining classes of casinos. As a result, casino premises licences are divided into three types:

- Regional casino premises licences;

- Large casino premises licence;

- Small casino premises licence

Section 151: Form of licence

411. Premises licences must include the information described in this section. The Secretary of State may make further regulations about the form and content of the licence. These regulations may, in particular, specify how conditions, including mandatory conditions specified by the Secretary of State, are to appear on the licence.

412. In Scotland, the powers of the Secretary of State in relation to the form of the licence are to be carried out by the Scottish Ministers.

Section 152: Combined licence

413. The general position for premises licensing is that premises may only be subject to one premises licence at a time. *Subsection (1)* provides for this. The effect of this requirement is to limit the principal activity on the premises to the provision of facilities for a particular type of gambling activity.

414. However, there are some exceptions to this approach. One exception is set out in this section. *Subsections (2) and (3)* provide that a betting track may be subject to more than one premises licence, but that no more than one premises licence can operate in relation to any area of the track. *Subsection (4)* provides that where a particular area of a track is already subject to a premises licence, and a person wishes to apply for a licence to offer another type of gambling activity in that area, an application must be made to vary the original licence under section 187. The new licence for the track can only be granted at the same time as, or after, the original licence has been varied. Other sections in this Part give permission for particular kinds of premises licence to authorise more than one type of activity.

Section 153: Principles to be applied

415. This section sets out the principles that licensing authorities should apply when exercising their premises licensing functions under this Part. They must to aim to permit the use of premises for gambling, in so far as the authority thinks that permission:

- accords with relevant Commission codes of practice and guidance under sections 24 and 25;

- is reasonably consistent with the licensing objectives; and

- is in accordance with the authority's three-year licensing policy (established by the authority under section 349 of the Act).

416.   Under legislation repealed by this Act, it has been a requirement that the grant of certain gambling permissions should take account of whether there is unfulfilled demand for the facilities. This is the case, for example, for a casino licence under Part II of the Gaming Act 1968 or a bookmaker's permit under the Betting, Gaming and Lotteries Act 1963. Unmet demand is not to be a criterion that a licensing authority is permitted to take into account when considering an application for a premises licence, and *subsection (2)* provides for this.

Section 154: Delegation to licensing committee
417.   With respect to England and Wales, this section provides that, with three exceptions, the functions of licensing authorities under Part 8 are delegated to the licensing committees established under section 6 of the Licensing Act 2003 (c.17). The three exceptions are:

- Functions relating to resolutions by the licensing authority not to issue casino licences under section 166;

- Formulation of the three year licensing policy under section 349; and

- Determination of premises licence fees under section 212.

The first two matters are not, and cannot be, delegated to a licensing committee, and must be taken by the authority as a whole. Decisions on fees are not automatically delegated, but can be.

418.   Section 10(4) of the Licensing Act 2003 limits the matters that may be delegated to an officer of the authority. In relation to gambling functions, under *subsection (4)* the matters that may not be delegated to an officer are:

- Determination of an application for a premises licence or a provisional statement in respect of which representations have been made under section 161 and have not been withdrawn;

- Determination of an application for of a premises licence in respect of which representations have been made under section 161 by virtue of section 187 and not withdrawn; or of an application for transfer of a licence following representations by the Commission;

- Review of a premises licence.

Section 155: Delegation of functions under Part 8: Scotland

419.   This section provides that, in relation to Scotland, the functions of licensing authorities may be delegated to a committee of the authority, a member or members of the authority, the clerk of the authority, or any person appointed to assist the clerk.

420.   The three exceptions to this are:

- Resolutions by the licensing authority not to issue casino licences under section 166;

- Formulation of the three year licensing policy under section 349; and

- The matters listed in *subsection (4)* of section 154.

421.   The first two matters may not be delegated at all, but the third matter may be delegated to a committee of the authority, or to a member or members of the authority.

422.   In Scotland, licensing authorities are licensing boards established under section 1 of the Licensing (Scotland) Act 1976. The procedures that apply to the proceedings of licensing boards in the exercise of their functions under that Act apply to the proceedings of those boards in relation to their functions under this Part. Regulations made by the Scottish Ministers dealing with the proceedings of licensing boards may make separate provision for the functions of the boards under the Licensing (Scotland) Act and under this Part.

Section 156: Register

423.   Under this section, licensing authorities must maintain a register of premises licences they have granted in their area, together with such other information as may be prescribed in regulations made by the Secretary of State. This register and information must be made available for inspection by the public. Licensing authorities must also provide a copy of an entry to the register, or of information, to a member of public on request, although they may charge for this service.

424.   The section also provides that the Secretary of State may, by regulations, require licensing authorities to give the Commission specified information about premises licenses issued by them; and may require the Commission to maintain a register and grant public access to it. Regulations made under this section may also excuse licensing authorities from part or all of their duties to maintain a register and provide access to it.

Section 157: Responsible authorities

425.   This section lists the people who are to be regarded as responsible authorities for the purposes of this Part. As responsible authorities they have particular rights to be involved and/or consulted in relation to applications for premises licences and other procedures under this Part. The Commission is a responsible authority, as are

the police.

Section 158: Interested party

426. In addition to responsible authorities, a wider group of people may play a role in the premises licensing process under this Part. These people are called "interested parties", and are defined in this section. Interested parties are:

- people who live sufficiently close to premises in respect of which a premises licence has been granted or applied for, that they are likely to be affected by activities authorised by the licence; and

- those with business interests who might be affected by the authorised activities; or

- representatives of either of these groups.

Sections 159 to 161: Applications

427. These sections prescribe the procedure for making an application for a premises licence. Only people with a right to occupy premises are eligible to apply for a premises licence. The notes relating to prize gaming permits under Part 14 expand upon the meaning of "occupy" for these purposes. Applicants must have an operating licence, or have made an application for one. A premises licence will not be issued until to an applicant until he holds an operating licence. The exception to this is an applicant for a premises licence that authorises a track to be used for accepting bets. These applicants do not need to hold, or have applied for, an operating licence.

428. Applications for premises licences must be made to the licensing authority in whose area the premises are wholly or partly situated; and must be in the prescribed form and manner, accompanied by the prescribed fee. Other sections in this Part describe the fee-setting powers relevant to premises licences.

429. The Secretary of State is given the power to make regulations which require an applicant for a premises licence to publish notice of his application, to give notice of it to responsible authorities and other people.

430. Responsible authorities and interested parties may make representations in writing to a licensing authority about a particular application. The period of time within which representations must be made will be prescribed in regulations.

431. Scottish Ministers exercise the powers of the Secretary of State under these sections in relation to Scotland.

432. Additional procedures apply in the case of applications for a casino licence. These are provided for in section 175 and Schedule 9.

Sections 162 to 165: Determination of application

433. These sections set out the procedure for determining an application. The

procedures vary, depending on whether representations have been made, and what the licensing authority proposes to do with regard to licence conditions.

434.   Where representations have been made by a responsible authority or an interested party (and not been withdrawn); or the licensing authority proposes to impose conditions on the licence, or exclude default conditions, a licensing authority is required to hold a hearing. The licensing authority may determine the application without a hearing, however, if either the applicant or any interested party has consented; or if the licensing authority considers that the representations made are vexatious, frivolous, or concern matters that will not influence their decision. Where the authority proposes to determine an application without a hearing, it must notify any person who made a representation as soon as reasonably practicable.

435.   Following the grant or rejection of a premises licence, the authority must notify the applicant, the Commission, any person who made representations, the police, and HM Customs and Excise of their decision as soon as reasonably practicable.

436.   Where the licensing authority determines to grant the licence, they must give reasons for the attachment or exclusion of any conditions. The premises licence issued by the licensing authority must be accompanied by a summary of the terms and conditions attaching to it. Where the licence is refused, the licensing authority must give reasons for their decision.

437.   Sections 206 to 209 set out the appeal rights in relation to a decision of a licensing authority to grant or reject an application for a premises licence. Where the licensing authority rejects an application for a licence, the applicant may appeal. Where the licensing authority grants an application, a person who made representations may appeal.

Section 166: Resolution not to issue casino licence
438.   Part 8 requires licensing authorities to permit the use of premises for gambling, in so far as the authority thinks that permission accords with relevant Commission codes of practice and guidance, is reasonably consistent with the licensing objectives, and is in accordance with the authority's three-year licensing policy (established by the authority under Part 18 of the Act).

439.   This section provides an exception to this requirement. Licensing authorities are given the power to decide not to issue further casino premises licences in their area. This decision is to be taken by the licensing authority as a whole, and may not be delegated to the licensing committee under sections 154 and 155. The licensing authority may take into account any principle or matter in making its decision, and may pass a resolution giving effect to their decision at any time. Such a resolution must be published as part of the authority's licensing policy statement made under Part 18, and lasts for 3 years from the date it takes effect.

440.   There are a number of restrictions on the scope of a resolution, as follows:

- A resolution can only apply to the grant of <u>future</u> applications for casino premises licences;

- It cannot have any effect on casino licences that have already been granted, (including licences that have been converted into casino licences or issued under transitional provisions under Part 18);

- It cannot have effect in relation to a provisional statement that has already been granted for a casino;

- A resolution must apply to all types of casino premises licence (e.g. regional, large and small); and

- A resolution may not be taken into account when reviewing a casino licence.

441.   Subsections 7 and 8 provide the Secretary of State with the power to order a particular licensing authority, or class of licensing authority to consider whether to issue a resolution under this section. Such an order may require, amongst other things, the authority to consult people likely to be affected by the resolution.

Sections 167 to 171: Conditions
442.   These sections provide the Secretary of State, Scottish Ministers and licensing authorities with powers to place conditions on premises licences.

443.   The Secretary of State and the Scottish Ministers have power to issue **mandatory** conditions on premises licences, for England and Wales, and Scotland respectively. Such conditions will be specified in regulations, and must be included in all premises licences, or classes of premises licence, to which they apply. These powers can apply to all premises licences, or classes of licence or to licences in specified circumstances.

444.   The Secretary of State and Scottish Ministers have further powers to impose **default** conditions by regulations, for England and Wales, and Scotland respectively. These conditions are ones which apply to a licence unless the licensing authority decides to exclude them (in which case the authority can impose alternative conditions relating to the same matter). These powers can apply to all premises licences, or classes of licence, or to licences in specified circumstances.

445.   In addition, licensing authorities have power to set individual conditions for a premises licence when they grant it. In doing so, they may impose a condition on a licence, or exclude default conditions (in which case they may impose alternative conditions relating to the same matter). Their power to impose conditions is subject to the matters listed below.

446.   A premises licence not may be subject to a condition imposed by a licensing

authority:

- that would prevent compliance with a condition on an operating licence which authorises the gambling activity (section 169(4));

- that requires the premises, or any part of it, to operate as a club or another body requiring membership (section 170);

- that imposes limits on stakes, fees, winnings or prizes (except in relation to fees for admission to a track) (section 171).

Section 172: Gaming machines

447.   Part 10 of the Act defines a gaming machine, and gives the Secretary of State power to make rules about their categorisation and use or manufacture and supply. This section contains the gaming machine entitlements which apply to the different types of premises licence issued under this Part. Licensing authorities may not vary these entitlements.

448.   The entitlements are:

- Adult gaming centres: up to four Category B machines and any number of Category C and D machines;

- Licensed family entertainment centres: any number of machines of Category C or D;

- Casinos:

    - Small casinos: 2 machines per gaming table used in the casino, up to a maximum of 80 machines. Machines may be of Category B,C or D;
    - Large casinos: 5 machines per gaming table used in the casino, up to a maximum of 150 machines. Machines may be of Category B, C or D;
    - Regional casinos: 25 machines per gaming table used in the casino, provided there are at least 40 tables, and up to a maximum of 1250 machines. Machines may be of Category A, B, C or D. If a regional casino has fewer than 40 tables, its entitlement is that of a large casino.

- Bingo premises: up to 4 Category B gaming machines, and any number of machines of Category C and D;

- Betting premises: up to 4 gaming machines of Category B, C or D;

- Tracks: Where the track licensee is permitted to offer pool betting: up to 4 machines of Category B, C or D.

449.   The Secretary of State may amend these entitlements in secondary legislation.

450.   In relation to casino entitlements, the Secretary of State can make regulations defining "gaming table", and, in particular may specify when a gaming table is to be treated as being used in a casino. These regulations could cover matters such as

whether appropriate numbers of staff are trained to operate the tables, and the extent to which such staff (and therefore tables) are available for use.

451.   These regulations can also specify when tables, which are linked together by electronic means for example, are to count as a single table for the purpose of machine entitlements under this section. This could be the case where one roulette wheel is operated by a croupier, but a number of associated banks of terminals allow players to take part in the game. The regulations will determine whether the banks of terminals count as a table in their own right. Part 10 of the Act contains provisions on when such equipment counts as a gaming machine.

Section 173: Virtual gaming
452.   This section authorises the provision of facilities for "virtual" betting in casinos and on betting premises. Section 353(3) contains a definition of "virtual" for these purposes.

Section 174: Casino premises licence
453.   Casino premises licences will be available for "small", "large" and "regional" casinos and will authorise the playing of casino games and equal chance games on the premises. Relevant definitions of these terms are set out in Part 1.

454.   A casino premises licence will also authorise the provision of facilities for betting, where the licensee or a person authorised in writing by the licensee holds a relevant betting operating licence. Large and regional casino premises licences also authorise the provision of facilities for bingo, again, provided there is a valid bingo operating licence held by the person providing the activity. Provision of facilities for bingo may not be made in a small casino, but the Secretary of State has power to repeal this restriction by order.

455.   *Subsection (6)* allows the Secretary of State to make regulations that impose mandatory conditions on casino premises licences in relation to equipment used for playing automated games of chance. Such equipment, which neither involves nor is linked to a game requiring human operation, is not a gaming machine provided it is used in accordance with Commission licence conditions set under this subsection (section 235(2)(i)). An example of this equipment is a roulette wheel which is completely mechanised, and works without the need for any croupier to rotate the wheel, spin the ball or accept stakes. Conditions may, in particular, limit the number of machines that may be provided in a casino and the number of player positions that may be provided for use of the machines.

456.   *Subsection (7)* allows the Secretary of State to use her powers via regulation to control the non-gambling facilities provided in casinos by attaching licence conditions. This does not prevent the licensing authority imposing conditions on such matters under section 169, subject to any mandatory conditions which the Secretary of State may prescribe under section 167.

Section 175: Casino premises licence: overall limits

457. This section sets an initial limit of 1 regional casino, and 8 small and 8 large casinos. The Secretary of State will, by order, determine the locations of the new casinos after consulting Scottish Ministers and the Welsh Assembly. The Secretary of State may by order vary the limits on the numbers of different categories of casino, or lift the limits altogether. Orders under this section are subject to the affirmative resolution procedure.

Schedule 9: Applications for casino premises licences

458. Schedule 9 sets out the process by which an operator may obtain a casino premises licence where there is a limit on the number of the particular category of casino.

459. As a first step a licensing authority must comply with regulations made by the Secretary of State about inviting competing applications. Where that leads to a number of applications, which is greater than the number of available premises licences, a two-stage process is to take place in accordance with *paragraphs 4 and 5*. Under paragraph 4, the first stage of the process is for the licensing authority to undertake a regulatory test on all the applications to ensure that they all satisfy the regulatory premises licensing requirements already contained in Part 8 of the Act. The second stage of the process, described in *paragraph 5*, only applies if more applicants pass this test than the number of available premises licences. In those circumstances, the licensing authority will run a competition to determine which of the competing applications, if successful, would offer the greatest benefits to the local area. *Paragraph 6* requires licensing authorities, in running this competition, to comply with any code of practice issued by the Secretary of State. *Paragraph 7* enables any commitments entered into by the successful applicant during the competition to be attached as conditions to the premises licence.

460. *Paragraph 8* makes provision for appeals against decisions of licensing authorities under paragraph 4. By virtue of *paragraph 8(4)* no appeal may be brought against a decision of a licensing authority under paragraph 5. *Paragraphs 9 and 10* make provision for the issuing of provisional statements, including allowing licensing authorities to set a time limit on the duration of a provisional statement.

Section 176: Casino premises licence: access by children

461. Under section 47 it is an offence to invite or permit children and young people to enter small or large casinos or the gambling area of a regional casino. Under this section the Commission must issue one or more codes of practice with respect to the arrangements which the holders of casino premises licences are to take to ensure that children and young people do not enter any areas where access is prohibited by virtue of section 47.

462. The codes or codes must also require that each entrance to prohibited areas is supervised (by one or more persons required to ensure compliance with the code of practice); and, unless the person supervising the entrance is reasonably certain that a

person wishing to enter is an adult, must require arrangements to be put in place which require the person seeking to enter to show evidence of their age. The type of evidence that is acceptable for proof of age is also to be set out in the code or codes of practice.

463. *Subsection (3)* makes it a condition of all casino premises licences that the licensee ensures compliance with a code of practice issued in accordance with *subsection (1)*.

Section 177: Credit

464. Section 81 contains restrictions on the holders of bingo and casino operating licences giving, arranging, permitting or knowingly facilitating credit in connection with the facilities for gambling they provide. This section contains equivalent provisions for the holders of casino and bingo premises licences. This ban on credit extends to any gambling facilities offered on the premises, because the holder of the premises licence must not permit or knowingly facilitate the giving of credit to take place on those premises. This therefore covers, for example, the provision of facilities for betting in a casino, pursuant to a betting operating licence and section 174(3). It will be a breach of the premises licence for credit to be offered in contravention of this section.

465. *Subsection (3)* contains an exception for cash withdrawal machines operated by credit card, located on the premises, in similar terms to the exception set out in section 81(3) and described in the note for that section.

Section 178: Door supervision

466. Where the Secretary of State or a licensing authority places a condition for door supervision on a premises licence, this will require entry to the premises to be supervised in order to prevent unauthorised access or occupation, outbreaks of disorder, or damage. Where such a condition is imposed, it a requirement of this section that the person undertaking the door supervision is licensed under the Private Security Industry Act 2001 (c.12), where his conduct is licensable under that Act.

467. Schedule 16, at paragraph 17 makes minor amendments to the 2001 Act, which preserve the exemption from licensing afforded to bingo and casino operators under that Act.

Section 179: Pool betting on track

468. Under the Betting, Gaming and Lotteries Act 1963, occupiers of licensed dog-tracks and the Totalisator Board ("the Tote") at approved horse racecourses enjoy certain exclusive rights to conduct pool betting on the races taking place there. These are the only tracks where pool betting is permitted. This section replaces those provisions in the 1963 Act.

469. Under *subsection (1)* the only tracks where pool betting is permitted, pursuant to a track betting premises licence, are dog tracks and horse racecourses. However,

the Secretary of State may amend this by order, and add further types of track, or remove them (*subsection (3)*). So, for example, football stadium could be added to the list, by order.

470.   On licensed dog tracks and horse racecourses, the holder of the track betting premises licence is given the exclusive right to offer pool betting on dog-racing or horse-racing respectively. He may authorise other people to conduct such pool-betting on his behalf. In all cases a relevant operating licence will be required. Track betting premises licences for dog tracks and horserace courses will be subject to mandatory licence conditions requiring access to be offered at the track-side to general betting operators. A licence condition will also be imposed for a transitional period, limiting the admission fee that can be charged to five times the public admission fee.

471.   There is no longer any special procedure for the licensing of inter-track betting schemes for dog racing (section 16A of the 1963 Act). Pool betting operating licences (which may be held for remote operations) and the track premises licence will cover, between them, all the activities that could be carried on under an inter-track licence.

Section 180: Pool betting on dog races

472.   This section contains a transitional measure for holders of dog-track betting premises licences. Holders of all betting premises licences (other than for a dog-track) may not permit pool betting on dog races to take place on their premises, unless it is in accordance with arrangements made with the occupier of the dog track on which the races take place. This means that a high street betting office cannot be used for pool betting on dog racing, unless it is covered by arrangements made between that office, and the relevant dog-track.

473.   The Secretary of State can repeal this measure, and, in any event, the section lapses after 31st December 2012.

Section 181: Betting machines

474.   Conditions attached to betting premises licences and casino premises licences may relate to the number of machines on the premises used for making or accepting bets; the nature of those machines and the circumstances of their use.

475.   This provision is relevant to machines used for making or accepting bets on real events. Such machines are excluded from the definition of gaming machine in Part 10 of the Act. Another section in this Part imposes restrictions on the number of gaming machines that may be made available for use on licensed premises, and this section enables similar restrictions to be imposed on machines used for making or accepting bets on real events. Likewise, there is an express regulation making power for controlling the use of gaming machines in Part 10, and this section enables similar controls to be imposed on real betting machines.

Section 182: Exclusion of children from track areas

476.   It is a mandatory condition of premises licences in relation to a track that

children and young people are to be excluded from any area where betting facilities are provided, or gaming machines, other than Category D machines, are made available for use. The exclusion from an area where betting facilities are provided does not apply to a dog-racing track or horse-racing track on a day on which racing takes place or is expected to take place. For the purposes of this section, an area where facilities are provided or a machine is situated is a place where it is possible to take advantage of the facilities or to use the machine.

477. The Secretary of State has the power to alter the places that children and young people are excluded from, and the circumstances in which they may be permitted access.

Section 183: Christmas Day

478. This section imposes a condition on all premises licenses that the premises shall not be used to provide facilities for gambling on Christmas Day.

Section 184: Annual fee

479. A premises licence holder must pay a fee to the licensing authority upon the grant of the licence, and annually thereafter. The Secretary of State (and, in Scotland, the Scottish Ministers) will prescribe in regulations the amount of the fee, and the period within which the initial fee must be paid. Such regulations may make different provisions for different classes of licences and different circumstances. Further provision for the setting of premises licence fees in England and Wales is made later in this Part.

480. The section also makes provision for the Secretary of State, or in Scotland, the Scottish Ministers, to set fees for circumstances where a premises licence is altered (following, for example, a change of circumstances, a variation, transfer or review) and, as a consequence, a different annual fee (either more or less than the original) is applicable.

Section 185: Availability of licence

481. Holders of premises licences must keep a copy of their licence on the premises and make it available to a police constable, a Commission enforcement officer or an authorised local authority officer. Failure to present the licence without reasonable excuse when requested by such people is an offence, for which the maximum penalty will be a fine of level 2 on the standard scale.

Section 186: Change of circumstance

482. The licence holder commits an offence if he fails to inform the licensing authority if his home or business address (on the licence) changes, or where another change of a type specified in regulations by the Secretary of State takes place. If, because of the change, information on the licence is rendered incorrect then the licence holder must send, with his notification, his licence (or an application for a copy of it under section 190), and the prescribed fee. The licensing authority will then alter the licence and send it back, or issue a copy in a form that reflects the change in

circumstance. If a person fails to comply with the requirements of this section, or the regulations made under it, he commits an offence. The penalty is a fine not exceeding level 2.

Section 187: Application to vary licence

483.   Licensees may apply to the licensing authority for a variation to their licence which will alter the authorised activities, change the conditions of the licence, or alter some other detail of the licence. A licence may not be varied so that it relates to premises to which it did not previously relate.

484.   The procedures in this Part for licence applications will apply to procedures for variation; however, the Secretary of State may make regulations providing for different procedures, including different procedures for different types of variation. These powers may be used to provide that a different fee applies for applications for variation from that which applies in respect of applications for a licence.

485.   An application for variation must be accompanied by the licence and a statement of the variation requested. If the licence cannot be provided, a statement explaining why the licence cannot be provided and an application for a copy must accompany the application.

Sections 188 & 189: Transfer

486.   Unlike operating licences, premises licences can be transferred, provided the transfer is to another operating licence holder (except in the case of betting premises licences in respect of tracks, where the transfer can be to any person). The procedures under this Part for premises licence applications will apply to applications for transfer with any necessary modifications. A different fee may be prescribed in relation to applications for transfer to that which applies in relation to an application for a licence.

487.   Where a licensing authority grants the application for transfer, it must alter the licence so that the applicant for transfer becomes the licensee; specify in the licence the time at which the transfer takes place; and make any alteration that appears to them to be required. This includes an alteration to attach or remove any condition.

488.   Where a licence has a condition attached in order to give effect to an agreement made for the provision of services by the licensee in the context of a competition for a casino premises licence under Schedule 9, that licence cannot be transferred unless the transferee enters into an new agreement that appears to the licensing authority to have substantially the same effect as the original agreement. The condition of the licence to which the agreement relates must then be altered to reflect the new agreement.

489.   Applications for transfer must state when the transfer is to take place and be accompanied by a written statement from the existing licence holder consenting to the transfer. It is possible for a transfer application to proceed without such a statement if

the applicant has been unable to contact the existing licence holder, having taken all reasonable steps to do so. In such circumstances the licensing authority may disapply the requirement for consent from the licence holder and take all reasonable steps to notify the existing licence holder of their decision.

490.   The licence or an application for a copy of the licence must accompany the application. Where the existing licensee is not contactable, the licence will be treated as being lost, stolen or damaged and the applicant must apply for a copy under section 190.

491.   If the application for transfer so requests, the applicant will be treated as though he were the licensee from the point that the application is received by the licensing authority to the determination of the application by the licensing authority.

492.   Regulations can be made to require an applicant for transfer to publish or give notice of his application to responsible authorities and other people specified. A responsible authority may make representations about the application to the licensing authority.

493.   A licensing authority will grant an application for transfer, unless they think it would be wrong to do so having regard to any representations that have been made. Decisions made under this section will be subject to rights of appeal by the licensee or the applicant for transfer.

Section 190: Copy of licence
494.   Where a premises licence, or summary of the terms and conditions, is lost, stolen or damaged, then the licence holder may apply to the licensing authority for a copy of the licence. The licensing authority must grant a copy if it is satisfied that the licence or summary has been lost, stolen or damaged and that the loss or theft has been reported to the police. A fee is payable, which will be set by the Secretary of State (and Scottish Ministers) in regulations. A copy of the licence or summary issued under this section shall be treated as though it were the original.

Section 191: Initial duration
495.   Premises licences are of unlimited duration, unless:

- the Secretary of State exercises powers under this section to impose a time limit on premises licences, or a class of premises licences, by secondary legislation.; or

- the licence ceases to have effect in accordance with other provisions in this Part.

496.   Regulations made by the Secretary of State under this section may have retrospective effect, and can make provision about renewals

Section 192: Surrender

497. Licensees may surrender their licences by writing to the licensing authority to give notice of their wish to do so, and enclosing the licence, or a written explanation of why it is not possible to provide the licence. The licensing authority must notify the surrender to the Commission, the police, and Her Majesty's Commissioners of Customs and Excise.

Section 193: Revocation for failure to pay fee

498. A premises licence will be revoked if the licence holder fails to pay the relevant annual fee (required under section 184), unless the failure to pay can be explained by an administrative error.

Section 194: Lapse

499. Where the licensee dies, becomes (in the opinion of the licensing authority) incapable of carrying out the licensed activities due to physical or mental incapacity; or becomes bankrupt; insolvent; ceases to exist; or goes into liquidation, then the licence will lapse. A lapsed licence may be reinstated under sections 195 and 196.

500. When a licensing authority becomes aware of the lapse of a licence, it must, as soon as reasonably practicable, notify the Commission, the police, and Her Majesty's Commissioners of Customs and Excise.

Sections 195 & 196: Reinstatement

501. For a period of 6 months beginning with the day on which the premises licence lapses, a person may apply for the licence to be reinstated in their name, instead of the person whose name is on the lapsed licence. The licence, or a statement of why the licence cannot be provided (along with an application for a copy of the licence), must accompany the application. The person seeking reinstatement must hold a relevant operating licence (except in the case of except in the case of betting premises licences in respect of tracks) in order for the licensing authority to be able to grant transfer. The requirements for licence applications are set out in section 159.

502. Regulations may be made requiring the applicant for reinstatement to publish or give notice of his application to certain specified (but not all) responsible authorities. A responsible authority may make representations about the application to the licensing authority.

503. The provisions in this Part relating to applications for premises licences apply to applications for reinstatement with any necessary modifications. The licensing authority will grant the application for reinstatement, unless they conclude that it would be wrong to do so, taking account of representations made by responsible authorities. On grant of the application, the licensing authority must alter the licence so that the applicant becomes the licensee; must specify that reinstatement take effect at the time when the application is granted; and must make any other alteration to the licence that they deem necessary.

504.   An applicant shall be treated as being the licensee during the period between the application for reinstatement being received by the licensing authority and the determination of that application.

505.   There is a right of appeal against the decision of the licensing authority to accept or reject an application for reinstatement under section 206.

Section 197: Application for review
506.   Under this Part, a premises licence may be reviewed:

- in response to an application to the licensing authority by a responsible authority or interested party (section 197); or

- on the initiation of the licensing authority (section 200).

507.   This section deals with applications by responsible authorities or interested parties. Applications must be in the form and manner prescribed by regulations made by the Secretary of State and Scottish Ministers. Regulations may also require an applicant to give notice of the application in a prescribed form and manner, to the licensee, and/or the responsible authorities in relation to the premises. In addition, the licensing authority may be required to publish notice of the application in the prescribed form and manner. Such notice must specify a period of time within which the licensee, a responsible authority or an interested party can make representations about the application.

Sections 198 & 199: Consideration of application
508.   Section 198 specifies the grounds on which a licensing authority may reject an application for a review made by a responsible authority or an interested party. They include that the application is frivolous or vexatious, or that it does not raise any new grounds to those previously raised during the original consideration of the grant of relevant premises licence, or on a previous application for review of that licence. An application for review can also be rejected because it does not raise any issue which is relevant to the principles which the authority is required to consider in granting a premises licence application.

509.   In determining whether to reject an application for a review, the licensing authority must consider the length of time that has elapsed since the last review and/or the grant of the relevant premises licence.

510.   If the licensing authority thinks that some of the grounds on which an application for a review may be rejected apply, they may reject the relevant parts of the application for the review. To the extent that a licensing authority does not reject an application for review, they must, under section 199, accept it.

Section 200: Initiation of review by licensing authority

511.   Where a review is initiated by a licensing authority, the authority may:

- review a particular class of premises licences, to assess the use of those premises or the arrangements made to ensure compliance with licence conditions (*subsection (1)*); or

- review a particular premises licence, where it suspects that the premises have not been used in accordance with a condition of a licence, or if it thinks that a review would be appropriate for any other reason. Before conducting such a review, the licensing authority must give notice of its intention to review the licence to the affected licensee, and also publish its intention.

512.   The Secretary of State may specify the form and manner of the notice of intention to review, and also the period of time within which notice is to be given. Where such regulations are made, they must specify a period of time within which representations about the review may be made by the licensee, a responsible authority or an interested party.

Sections 201 to 203: Review

513.   Where a licensing authority has granted an application for a review, or has given notice of its intention to initiate a review, it must review the licence as soon as reasonably practicable (after the period for giving representations has expired) in order to determine what, if any, action should be taken under this Part.

514.   In conducting the review, the licensing authority must hold a hearing unless the applicant for the review and any person who made representations has consented to the hearing being waived; or the licensing authority considers that all the representations made following notice of the review are frivolous, vexatious or will not influence their decision.

515.   When determining what, if any, action under section 202(1) to take, the licensing authority must take into account representations made before or during the hearing, and the grounds specified in any application for a review made by a responsible authority or an interested party.

516.   Following a review, a licensing authority may:

- suspend (for a period not exceeding 3 months) or revoke a licence; or

- amend, add or exclude the conditions attached to the licence. This includes reinstating a condition imposed under section 168 that they excluded under section 169.

517.   After completing a review of a licence, the licensing authority must notify the licensee, the applicant for a review (if any), the Commission, any person who made representations, the police and Customs and Excise of their decision as soon as

possible after it has been made. Notification must give reasons for the decision.

518.   A right of appeal is provided against a determination by the licensing authority to take, or not to take, action under these sections. An appeal may be made by the licensee; any person who made representations in relation to a review; the person (if any) who applied for the review; and the Commission.

Sections 204 & 205: Provisional statement

519.   Where a person expects premises to be constructed or altered, or expects to acquire a right to occupy premises, he may apply for a provisional statement from the licensing authority, in advance of a full premises licence.

520.   Subject to any necessary modifications, the provisions relating to applications for premises licences under this Part apply to applications for provisional statements. A person does not require a right to occupy the premises, or an operating licence in order to be granted a provisional statement.

521.   An application for a provisional statement must include plans, and information in relation to the construction, alteration or acquisition of property as may be prescribed by the Secretary of State in regulations.

522.   Where granted, the provisional statement offers a degree of certainty to the applicant when he comes to apply for a premises licence because, unless the property has not been constructed or altered in accordance with the plans submitted to the licensing authority, when considering the application for the premises licence:

- the licensing authority must disregard any representations made, except where they relate to matters that could not have been addressed in relation to the application for a provisional statement; or where they reflect a change of circumstances relating to the applicant; and

- the licensing authority may only refuse the application for the premises licence or impose conditions not included in the provisional statement, by taking into account matters which are valid representations (as defined above) or where there has been a change in the circumstances of the applicant.

523.   An example of a change in an applicant's circumstances that might be relevant may be where the applicant has been convicted of a relevant offence following his application for a provisional statement; such that the applicant is now unable to get an operating licence.

524.   If the property in respect of which the application has been made has been altered or constructed in a way that is not in accordance with the plans that were submitted with the application for a provisional statement, the licensing authority are not limited in their consideration of the application for the premises licence in the

ways outlined above.

525. Where a provisional statement is granted in respect of a casino premises, under Schedule 9, *paragraphs 9 and 10*, the licensing authority may specify a time period for which it is to have effect. In such a case, the period may be extended by the licensing authority on application by the holder.

Sections 206 to 209: Rights of Appeal

526. These sections set out which licensing authority decisions under this Part are subject to appeal, and by whom. They include a decision to reject or grant an application (including rejection or grant of an application to reinstate a licence, and an application for a provisional statement); a decision whether to take action as a result of a review; and a decision whether to transfer a licence. In addition, Schedule 9 provides that an applicant may appeal against a decision to impose a time limit on the period for which a provisional casino premises licence applies.

527. Appeals under this Part must be made, in England and Wales, to the magistrates' court within 21 days of the relevant decision. Unless he is the appellant, the licence holder or applicant, as the case may be, must be joined as a respondent in addition to the licensing authority.

528. The magistrates may dismiss the appeal, substitute a new decision that could have been made by the licensing authority, remit the case back to the licensing authority, and also make an order about costs. Where the case is remitted, there is a further right of appeal on the same terms. In Scotland, appeals will be made to the sheriff on the same terms, except that there will be no right for the sheriff to substitute his own decision.

529. Any determination or action under this Part will be stayed during an appeal, or during the period within which an appeal could have been brought, unless the licensing authority, when making a determination or taking action, directs otherwise (in which case the magistrates' court or sheriff may make any appropriate order). There is a further right of appeal on a point of law to the High Court in England and Wales, or the Court of Session in Scotland.

Section 210: Planning permission

530. This section makes it clear that a licensing authority is not to have regard to planning or building law matters when considering an application under Part 8. It also provides that any decision on the application by a licensing authority is not to constrain a later decision by the authority under planning or building law.

Section 211: Vessels and vehicles

531. This section provides that premises licences may be granted to passenger vessels, but may not be granted to vehicles. The interpretation section in Part 18 contains provisions for defining vessels and vehicles, and this section contains rules for determining where vessels are located for the purpose of applying for a premises

licence. Section 359 defines the territorial limitations on the Act in relation to vessels.

532.   Where an application for a premises licence is made in respect of a vessel, the bodies listed in *subsection (4)* will be responsible bodies, with the same rights as responsible authorities generally under this Part.

533.   The effect of this section (together with other provisions in the Act in relation to vehicles) is that gaming and betting on vehicles is unlawful under the Act, unless the gambling constitutes private gaming or betting within the meaning of Part 14 and Schedule 15. Section 360 defines the territorial limitations on the Act in relation to aircraft.

534.   Schedule 11 contains rules on the lawful promotion of exempt lotteries on vessels. Permits under Schedules 10, 12 and 14 may not be granted to vessels or vehicles. Authorisations under Schedule 13 will be available for vessels and vehicles to the same extent that they are available to them under the Licensing Act 2003.

Section 212: Fees
535.   At a number of sections in this Part, provision is made for fees to be payable to licensing authorities, and for those fees to be set by the Secretary of State, or Scottish Ministers. Under this section, the Secretary of State may devolve to licensing authorities in England and Wales the freedom to set fees for premises licence applications relating to their area, subject to any constraints specified in the regulations.

536.   Where licensing authorities are given power to determine a fee:

*   they may set different fees for different classes of case specified in the regulations e.g. for different types of licence (but not otherwise); and

*   they must aim to ensure that the income from the fees they set equals (as nearly as possible) the costs of providing the particular services to which the fee relates. In determining whether this cost recovery principle is being met, licensing authorities may make a comparison between costs and fees over whatever period it considers to be appropriate. The Secretary of State may issue guidance to licensing authorities on the appropriate periods for comparison. Where she does so, the licensing authority must take account of that guidance.

537.   This permits the Secretary of State to set bands of minimum or maximum fees, within which a licensing authority can set its individual charges. Alternatively, the Secretary of State can give an authority complete discretion to set its own fees, subject always to the cost recovery principle.

538.   Regulations under this section need not apply to all licensing authorities in England and Wales and may, in particular, apply only to categories of authority. In England, such categorisation could be achieved by reference to categories

assigned under section 99 of the Local Government Act 2003 (c.26) (Comprehensive Performance Assessment).

539.   This section does not apply to Scotland.

PART 9: TEMPORARY USE OF PREMISES

540.   Part 9 makes provision for the use of premises for gambling where there is no premises licence in respect of those premises, but an operating licence holder wishes to use the premises, temporarily, for providing facilities for gambling.

541.   Temporary use notices, endorsed by licensing authorities, will authorise the provision of gambling activities temporarily on specific premises. The nature of the gambling activities that can be provided under such notices will be controlled by the Secretary of State in regulations. Examples of premises which could be subject to a temporary use notice are hotels, exhibition centres or entertainment venues.

542.   Part 1 defines the licensing authorities which will consider temporary use notices, and Part 18 requires licensing authorities to make a licensing policy statement in relation to their functions under this Part.

Sections 214 to 218: Temporary use notice
543.   Where an operating licence holder wishes to provide facilities for gambling temporarily on premises, he may give notice in writing (a "temporary use notice") that he intends to use the premises for the provision of facilities for gambling. Only a holder of an operating licence may give a temporary use notice, and the activity that he wishes to provide must be the same activity that he is authorised to provide facilities for under the terms of his operating licence.

544.   The temporary use notice must be in the form prescribed by the Secretary of State, and must specify the information listed in section 216(1).

545.   A temporary use notice cannot authorise any gambling activities. It can only authorise such gambling activities as the Secretary of State may specify in regulations, and which are set out in the notice. These regulations may also specify combinations of activities that may not be provided together under a temporary use notice. For example, if facilities for poker, blackjack and pool betting were to be authorised by the Secretary of State, a temporary use notice could not permit the provision of such facilities at the same time, on the same premises.

546.   Section 218 provides that a set of premises cannot be subject to a temporary use notices for more than 21 days in any 12 month period. This means that, while several different temporary use notices may have effect for a set of premises over a period of time, the aggregate period of these notices cannot exceed 21 days in a 12 month period. This is the case even if the gambling activities taking place under the

notices are different activities. The maximum period of 21 days applies to all gambling carried on pursuant to notices, not merely one type of gambling.

547. These sections set out procedures for the licensing authority to ensure that these time periods are complied with. If any notice is served which is in breach of these requirements, the authority must serve a counter-notice which prevents the temporary use notice authorising gambling for anything over the permitted 21 days.

548. A valid (i.e. endorsed) temporary use notice, which complies with the requirements of this Part, will authorise gambling carried on pursuant to it, and no offences under Part 3 of the Act will be committed.

Sections 219 & 220: Giving notice: procedure
549. A temporary use notice must be served upon a licensing authority for the area in which the premises are situated. It must be given at least three months before it is proposed to have effect. It must arrive with both the licensing authority and any other person entitled to receive it within 7 days of the date on which it is stated to have been given.

550. A number of procedural requirements must be followed, including the payment of any fee that is prescribed by the Secretary of in regulations. In England and Wales this fee setting power may be devolved to licensing authorities in accordance with section 212. In addition, the person giving notice must also give a copy of it to the Commission, the police, and Her Majesty's Commissioners of Customs and Excise. This allows these people to object to the proposed notice, as outlined below.

551. The licensing authority receiving a notice must acknowledge its receipt as soon as practicable thereafter.

Sections 221 to 223: Objections and modification by agreement
552. The licensing authority or anyone else entitled to receive a copy of a notice may object to it. The grounds for objections are that, having regard to the licensing objectives set out in Part 1 of the Act, the notice should not have effect, or should only have effect with modifications. A notice of objection must be served upon the person seeking to make the facilities for gambling available (i.e. the server of the temporary use notice) within 14 days of the date of the temporary use notice, and must state the reasons for the objection. A copy must also be given to the licensing authority.

553. Where objection notices have been served, the licensing authority must hold a hearing at which representations may be made by the person who gave the temporary use notice, the people who objected, and any other people who were entitled to receive a copy of the notice. This requirement may be waived if the licensing authority, and each person who would be entitled to make representations, agree in writing that a hearing is unnecessary.

554.   Where an objection has been made to a temporary use notice, but a hearing has not taken place (either because it has not yet happened, or because it has been dispensed with), anyone who has raised objections under these sections may propose a modification to the notice. If the modifications are agreed, a new temporary use notice, incorporating the modifications, can be served and the original notice will be treated as withdrawn. In these circumstances, the three-month time limit and fee will not apply to the new temporary use notice. If all objections are dealt with by modifications then this will dispense with the further need to hold a hearing in relation to the notice. If not, then those with objections outstanding can continue to contest the notice.

Sections 224 to 226: Counter-notices and dismissal of objections
555.   Where:

- an objection notice has been served;

- modification has not removed the objection; and

- either a hearing has taken place, or been dispensed with,

the licensing authority may determine that the temporary use notice should not have effect, or should only have effect with modifications. The principles it must apply in reaching a view are the same as those it applies when determining premises licence applications. Therefore, it should aim to permit the temporary use of premises for gambling, in so far as it thinks that permission:

- accords with relevant Commission codes of practice and guidance;

- is reasonably consistent with the licensing objectives; and

- is in accordance with the authority's three-year licensing policy (established by the authority under section 349 of the Act).

556.   If the authority concludes that the temporary use notice should not have effect, or should only have effect with modifications, it must serve a counter-notice upon the person who served the temporary use notice. This counter-notice may provide that the temporary use notice:

- will not have effect;

- will have effect only in respect of a certain activity;

- will only have effect in relation to an activity for a certain period of time or during certain hours of the day; or

- will be subject to a condition.

557.   A counter notice must be in the prescribed form and state the licensing authority's reasons for giving it. A copy must be given to any person who was entitled

to receive a copy of the temporary use notice under section 219.

558.   If the authority concludes that it will not give any counter-notice, then it must inform all relevant parties of this fact. The effect is that any objection notices have been dismissed by the authority.

559.   Rights of appeal are available following an authority's decision to issue a counter-notice or to dismiss objections under these sections. The person who gave the temporary use notice, and any person entitled to receive a copy of it, may appeal. An appeal lies to the magistrates' court, and must be made within 14 days of receiving notice of the licensing authority's decision. In Scotland, the appeal will be to the sheriff in whose area the premises are located. If the appeal is against the decision of the licensing authority not to issue a counter notice, then the person giving the temporary use notice will also be a respondent in the case.

560.   Where the decision to appeal may be made by a person entitled to receive a copy of the notice under section 219, they must decide whether to appeal, and to institute any appeal as soon as is reasonably practicable.

561.   The magistrates' court or sheriff may, on hearing an appeal, dismiss it; direct the licensing authority to take some specified action; remit it back to the licensing authority to decide in accordance with a direction of the court; and make an order as to costs (or expenses). Where the decision is remitted to the licensing authority, the same rights of appeal will flow from their new decision as applied to their original one.

562.   A further right of appeal exists to the High Court or Court of Session on a point of law.

Section 227: Endorsement of notice
563.   If no objections are raised to a temporary use notice during the 14-day period after it is made, then the licensing authority will return the notice to the person who gave it, endorsing it as valid. The Secretary of State may prescribe the precise method of endorsement in regulations.

564.   If a notice of objection was served, but did not result in a counter-notice being served (i.e. the objections were dismissed) then the temporary use notice must similarly be endorsed and returned, as soon as reasonably practicable, to the person who gave it.

565.   An endorsed temporary use notice provides authorisation for the specified facilities for gambling to be provided at the relevant premises, in accordance with its terms.

Section 228: Consideration by licensing authority: timing
566.   Licensing authorities will have six weeks from the date of the temporary use

notice to complete proceedings on the notice. This includes proceedings to consider whether to give a notice of objection; holding a hearing or agreeing to dispense with one, and giving a counter notice or a notice dismissing any objections.

Sections 229 & 230: Miscellaneous provisions

567.   An endorsed temporary use notice must be displayed on the premises to which it relates at any time when it is being relied upon. It must also be made available on request to a police constable, a Commission enforcement officer, an authorised local authority officer, or an officer of Her Majesty's Customs and Excise. If a person fails to display or produce his notice as required, he will commit an offence for which he will be liable to a fine not exceeding level 2 on the standard scale.

568.   A person who has given a temporary use notice to a licensing authority may withdraw it at any time. It will then cease to have effect and any proceedings relevant to it will cease, except in relation to a matter which arose during, or in relation to, any time during which it was in effect.

Section 231: Vehicles and vessels

569.   A temporary use notice may be given in respect of a passenger vessel, but may not be given in relation to a vehicle. The interpretation section in Part 18 contains provisions for defining vessels and vehicles, and this section contains rules for determining where vessels are located for the purpose of a licensing authority's functions under this Part. See also the note on section 211.

Section 232: Delegation of licensing authority functions: England and Wales

570.   This section provides that the provisions of Part 8 of the Act, in relation to the delegation of functions to a licensing committee established under the Licensing Act 2003, and further delegation to officers of the authority under sections 154 and 155, apply similarly to this Part. The only matter that may not be sub-delegated under this Part is the decision under section 224 to issue a counter notice. That decision must be made by the licensing committee.

Section 233: Delegation of licensing authority functions: Scotland

571.   This section provides that the provisions of Part 8 of the Act, in relation to the delegation of functions of Scottish licensing authorities, apply similarly to this Part. The decision to issue a counter-notice under this Part may not, however, be delegated to the clerk of the authority, or a person appointed to assist him.

Section 234: Register

572.   This section makes provision for licensing authorities to maintain a register of temporary use notices in a form and manner specified by the Secretary of State in regulations. The register must be available for inspection by members of the public at all reasonable times, and a copy must be provided to a member of the public on request. A charge may be made for copies.

573.   The Secretary of State may also, in regulations, require licensing authorities to

provide information about temporary use notices to the Commission in a specified fashion. The Commission may then be required to keep its own register of the information provided to it, and may relieve licensing authorities from the need to maintain a register under this section.

PART 10: GAMING MACHINES

574.   Part 10 contains the main provisions of the Act on gaming machines. It sets out a definition of "gaming machine" together with the offences relevant to illegal use or manufacture of a gaming machine. Parts 5 and 8 of the Act deal with certain authorisations and entitlements to use gaming machines that arise from operating or premises licences respectively. This Part provides general provisions which apply to the use of any gaming machine, and includes regulation-making powers for the Secretary of State to set categories of machine and rules on use.

575.   Manufacture, supply, maintenance, repair, installation and adaptation of a gaming machine are all regulated activities under this Part.

576.   This Part applies to any gaming machine situated in Great Britain, or anything done in Great Britain in relation to a gaming machine, wherever that machine is situated (section 251). For example, a gaming machine manufactured in Great Britain, for export to another country, will be covered by the provisions in Part 10. Accordingly, a gaming machine technical operating licence under Part 5 of the Act will be available to manufacturers and suppliers who wish to cater for the overseas market. Such machines need not comply with the categorisation regulations under section 236 if the machines are for export. Machines supplied for use in Great Britain will need to comply with the requirements of Part 10, even if manufactured abroad.

Section 235: Gaming machine
577.   This section provides a definition of a gaming machine for the Act. It is significantly broader than the definition of gaming machine in section 26 of the Gaming Act 1968, which the Act repeals. The new definition accommodates developments in technology which have taken place since the 1968 Act. It also covers a wide range of gambling activities which can take place on a machine, and includes betting on virtual events.

578.   *Subsection (1)* defines a gaming machine as a machine that is designed or adapted for use by people to gamble (whether or not it can be used for other purposes). This is a wide definition. *Subsection (3)(b)* contains further detail about how the words "designed or adapted" are to be interpreted, particularly in relation to a computer.

579.   *Subsection (2)* then sets out a number of exceptions to subsection (1) which ensure that the gaming machine definition does not capture certain specified types of

machine.

580.   The definition at subsection (1) does not depend on any concept of players depositing payments into the machine, or on the gambling activity being generated from within the machine itself (as opposed to being transmitted to the machine from other equipment). Nor is it restricted solely to gaming. To the extent that these were requirements under the 1968 Act, they are no longer part of the new definition.

581.   The exclusions at subsection (2) provide that the following are not gaming machines:

- A **domestic or dual-use computer** which can be used for participating in remote gambling. The Secretary of State will prescribe the meaning of "domestic computer" and "dual-use computer" in regulations. The purpose of this exception is to exempt internet terminals and home computer equipment, which are not dedicated or specifically configured for gambling activities, from the definition of gaming machine. The mere fact that a home computer can be used to access gambling facilities should not render the computer a gaming machine. However, someone offering the public access to the internet, via terminals, and configuring them to encourage gambling, is making a gaming machine available for use (unless any other exception applies, such as betting on real events). The regulations to be made under this power will set out the relevant criteria for determining whether equipment is a domestic or dual use computer, and can refer to matters such as the location of the computer, the software installed on the computer, and the circumstances in which the computer is used (*subsections (2)(a), (3)(f) and (4)*);

- A **telephone or other communications device** that can be used for remote gambling (other than a computer). The fact that, with modern technology, a telephone or interactive television can be used to participate in gambling will not render the equipment a gaming machine (*subsection (2)(b)*). This exception does not apply to computers;

- A **machine which is designed or adapted for betting only on future real events**. This exemption is designed to prevent equipment, such as automated betting terminals, through which people place bets on real, not virtual, events, from being counted as gaming machines. The event must be a future event at the time the machine is used, meaning that betting on pre-recorded activities, where the result is already known, is not exempt. The exempt equipment is not unregulated. Making it available as part of a business will be providing facilities for betting, and will require the relevant operating licences under the Act. However, in regulatory terms, these machines are not to be treated as gaming machines (*subsection (2)(c)*).

- A **machine upon which someone enters a lottery**. Provided that the machine does not determine the result of the lottery, or announces it only after a specified period, then such a machine is not a gaming machine. This means that if a machine only dispenses lottery tickets (for a draw that takes place completely independent of the machine), or vends lottery paper scratchcards, then the machine is outside the definition of a gaming machine. If the machine announces the results of the lottery, as well as selling tickets to it, then the machine will not be a gaming machine provided a prescribed interval has elapsed between the sale of the ticket and the announcement of the result. The Secretary of State will determine the duration of the period by order. In no circumstances can the machine determine the result of the lottery (*subsection (2)(d)*).

- A **machine for playing bingo** which is used by the holder of a bingo operating licence, in accordance with conditions attached by the Commission. This is designed to exempt what is known as "mechanised cash bingo equipment" which is used for playing real bingo games, but whose degree of computerisation or mechanisation means that it would otherwise be caught by the definition of gaming machine. The need for it to comply with Commission conditions ensures that the exemption is construed narrowly and not extended to any machine on which a virtual bingo game could be played (*subsection (2)(e)*);

- A **machine for playing bingo prize gaming** which is used by the holder of a gaming machine general operating licence (for an adult gaming centre or a family entertainment centre), in accordance with conditions attached to those licences by the Commission. This is designed to exempt equipment used for playing real prize bingo, in accordance with the terms of Part 13 of the Act. The need for it to comply with Commission conditions ensures that the exemption is construed narrowly and not extended to any machine on which a virtual bingo game could be played (*subsection (2)(f)*);

- A **machine for playing bingo prize gaming** which is used by an unlicensed family entertainment centre or pursuant to a prize gaming permit, in accordance with any Commission code of practice. This exemption is similar to that at subsection (2)(g), but applies to different types of operator who have prize gaming rights under Part 13 (*subsection (2)(g)*);

- A **machine which is used for playing manual games of chance.** This is a machine which:

  - is controlled or operated by someone employed to do so (e.g. a croupier spinning a roulette wheel); or
  - is used in connection with a real game of chance which is controlled or operated by an individual (e.g. a computer terminal for staking on the outcome of a roulette wheel that is spun by a croupier) (*subsection (2)(h)*).

In both these instances the equipment could be construed as a gaming machine under the broad definition, but the fact that it is operated as part of a real game of chance means that it is not to be regulated under the gaming machine provisions. Such equipment and activities will be regulated under other parts of the Act.

- **A machine which is used for playing automated games of chance in a**

casino. This is equipment used for playing a real game of chance, pursuant to a casino operating licence, but which has no human involvement from the organisers of the casino game, and which is not linked to a game which does have such human involvement. For example, apparatus such as a roulette wheel which is completely mechanised, and works without the need for any croupier to rotate the wheel, spin the ball or accept stakes. This equipment is not a gaming machine provided it is used in accordance with Commission licence conditions. Section 174(6) contains further provisions in relation to this equipment in casinos.

582.   These various exemptions prevent the broad definition of gaming machine from capturing equipment unintentionally.   The definition in subsection (1) is intended to cover a gaming machine that is used for taking part in virtual gaming, virtual betting or a virtual lottery (where the draw is part of the activity determined by the machine).

583.   *Subsection (3)* provides clarification about the characteristics of a gaming machine. Reference to part of a gaming machine includes computer software to be used in a gaming machine, but does not include a component of a gaming machine which does not influence the outcome of the gambling (*subsection (3)(c)*). This means that where a gaming machine technical operating licence is required for the manufacture, installation etc. of gaming machines, computer software intended for use in the machine is included within the licensing requirement. However, the plywood from which the machine is constructed is not. References to installing part of a gaming machine include installing computer software (*subsection (3)(d)*). This is required because machines can be configured or changed by the downloading of gambling software, without any need to physically interfere with the machine.

584.   *Subsection (5)* allows the Secretary of State to make regulations concerning the sub-division of apparatus into individual gaming machines. It is no longer the case that a gaming machine will take the form of a stand-alone machine in the form of a traditional "fruit-machine". A single computer can be linked to a number of player positions and offer each player the experience of playing a gaming machine, although the apparatus forms one large whole. To tackle the possibility of evasion of the Act's regulation for gaming machines, this power allows rules to be made for calculating when a single piece of apparatus counts as more than one machine, and, in particular, can focus on the number of player positions available. These regulations will supplement other parts of the Act, where numerical limits are placed on the entitlements to make gaming machines available for use.

Section 236: Gaming machines: Categories A to D
585.   Gaming machines will be divided into categories, with different entitlements set out in the Act to use the various categories. This section requires the Secretary of State to define, in regulations, four classes of gaming machine, to be known as categories A, B, C and D. Category B may also be sub-divided into further sub-categories, and these regulations may identify to which sub-category of B machine an

entitlement relates (*subsections (1) and (2)*).

586.   The categorisation will refer to the particular facilities for gambling which are offered on the machine.   In particular, *under subsection (4)*, the regulations can specify:

- the maximum amounts that can be paid to use the machine;

- the value or nature of the prize delivered as a result of its use;

- the nature of the gambling for which the prize is used; or

- the types of premises on which it can be used.

587.   These matters can be combined so that, for example, one category of machine could have different maximum use charges dependent on the nature of the prize offered by the machine.

588.   Details of the proposed A to D categorisation of gaming machines is set out in the Regulatory Impact Assessment published alongside the Act. The intention is that Category D will have the lowest levels of charge and prizes, and that these will increase in value, up to Category A, which will be a machine with no limits as to charges and prizes.

589.   Part 8 of the Act contains the principal commercial entitlements for different types of licensed gambling premises to use different categories of machines. Different permissions are also available under Part 12 of the Act, for clubs, miners' welfare institutes, alcohol licensed premises and travelling fairs, and, also, pursuant to this Part, for family entertainment centres.

Sections 237 to 239: Other definitions
590.   These sections set out definitions for an adult gaming centre, a family entertainment centre, (including a licensed family entertainment centre), and a "prize" in relation to a gaming machine.

Sections 240 & 241: Use and supply of machines
591.   The Secretary of State can make regulations about the way in which gaming machines can operate. It will be an offence to make a gaming machine available for use if the machine does not comply with such regulations.

592.   *Under subsection (2)*, the regulations may provide, in particular, for rules about:

- The method by which payment may be made for use of machine (i.e. whether coins, banknotes, smartcards, tokens or other methods can be used). It is a separate offence, under this Part, to supply, install or make a machine available which can be paid for by a credit card;

- The nature of, and arrangements, for receiving or claiming prizes;

- The rollover of stakes or prizes (i.e. the carry over of amounts paid or won to a subsequent use of the machine);

- The proportion of stakes or sums paid for use which must be returned as prizes;

- The display of information on or around the machine (e.g. information on minimum age of use); or

- Any other matter relating to the way that the machine works (e.g. whether it must operate randomly or not).

593.   The Secretary of State may also make regulations about the supply, installation, adaptation, maintenance or repair of a gaming machine.

594.   The penalty for making a machine available for use, in breach of these regulations, is a maximum term of imprisonment of 51 weeks in England and Wales, or 6 months in Scotland, or a fine up to level 5, or both.

595.   Regulatory steps taken by the Commission, and any licence conditions it sets, must not conflict with these regulations. The Secretary of State can also identify matters about which licence conditions cannot be made in relation to machines. The Commission is empowered in Part 5 to set standards for gaming machines under section 96, and regulation of gaming machines is therefore a dual function of both the Secretary of State, and the Commission.

Section 242: Making machine available for use
596.   The principal offence of making a gaming machine available for use unlawfully is set out in this section. A person will commit an offence if he makes any gaming machine available for use unless:

- He holds an operating licence which permits such use;

- He holds a family entertainment centre permit;

- He holds a club gaming permit or a club machine permit under Part 12;

- He has appropriate permission for alcohol licensed premises under Part 12;

- He makes gaming machines available at a travelling fair as permitted by Part 12, or;

- The machine offers no, or a limited, prize (as defined in this Part).

597.   Under Part 3 of the Act it is a separate offence for a person to use premises for making a gaming machine available for use without the necessary authorisation or exemption, such as a premises licence or a Category D gaming machine permit. It will also be an offence under this section to make a gaming machine available for use if the machine does not comply with regulations made by the Secretary of State under

section 240.

598.   The penalty for this offence is a maximum term of imprisonment of 51 weeks in England and Wales, or 6 months in Scotland, and/or a fine up to level 5.

Section 243: Manufacture, supply etc.

599.   As well as setting requirements about the use of machines, the Act stipulates that various activities concerning the manufacture or supply of a gaming machine must also be regulated by the Commission. Under Part 5 of the Act, gaming machine technical operating licences are available for those wishing to manufacture, supply, install, adapt, maintain or repair a gaming machine. Failure to hold such an operating licence, when undertaking any of these activities, is an offence under this section. The penalty is a maximum term of imprisonment of 51 weeks in England and Wales, or 6 months in Scotland, and/or a fine up to level 5.

600.   Exceptions from this offence exist:

*   for those holding a single machine supply and maintenance permit under this Part;

*   for machines exempted by regulations under section 248(2) (no prize);

*   where the activities relate to a gaming machine that is for scrap; or

*   where the supply is incidental to the sale or letting of a property.

601.   This means that no operating licence is required where a machine is being broken up and no further use is made of it for gaming machine purposes, and where the machines are ancillary to the sale of a business which uses gaming machines. Any use, after sale, will continue to be subject to the other requirements of the Act.

Section 244: Linked machines

602.   It is an offence, under this section, for gaming machines to be linked so that they operate together, and the value of the prize available on one machine is determined to any extent by use of the other machine. There is one exception to this, which is that *subsection (2)* permits machines to be linked at licensed casino premises provided that all of the machines are situated on the same premises. Linkage of gaming machines in this way does not authorise casino licensees to offer maximum prizes in excess of those allowed for the category of machine being used.

603.   No linking between licensed casino premises is permitted, but *subsection (3)* gives the Secretary of State power to lift this prohibition, subject to appropriate Parliamentary approval.

604.   The penalty, upon conviction for this offence, is a maximum term of imprisonment of 51 weeks in England and Wales, or 6 months in Scotland, or a fine up to level 5, or both.

Section 245: Credit

605.   It is an offence for a person to supply, install or make available a gaming machine which allows payment to be made by means of a credit card. The penalty, upon conviction for this offence, is a maximum term of imprisonment of 51 weeks in England and Wales, or 6 months in Scotland, or a fine up to level 5, or both.

Section 247: Family entertainment centre permits

606.   Family entertainment centre ("FEC") gaming machine permits allow certain gaming machines to be made available for use without an operating or premises licence. These permits are issued by licensing authorities using the procedure set out in Schedule 10. They relate to the lowest category of machine. If an FEC wished to use Category C and D machines, it would require an appropriate operating and premises licence, under Parts 5 and 8 of the Act. The permits provided for here only relate to Category D machines.

607.   Only premises which are wholly or mainly used for making gaming machines available for use may hold an FEC gaming machine permit. This is a change from the position prior to the Act, when any premises could apply for a permit allowing them to use an "amusements with prizes" gaming machine (the nearest equivalent to a Category D machine). The intention is that gaming machines in certain non-gambling premises, like those now sometimes located in fish and chip shops and taxi cab ranks, should be removed. Once these provisions are commenced, permits previously granted under Schedule 9 to the Gaming Act 1968 will no longer be available under the Act, except to the extent that they relate to premises wholly or mainly used for making gaming machines available for use. Transitional provisions, under Part 18, will give effect to this change, and allow existing permits to continue after the repeal of the relevant provisions of the 1968 Act, until the date on which they would otherwise have expired if those provisions had continued in force. The position of premises holding an alcohol licence is dealt with separately in Part 12.

Schedule 10: Family Entertainment Centre gaming machine permits

608.   This schedule sets out the procedures for the application for and grant of an FEC gaming machine permit by licensing authorities. It also regulates the permit's form and maintenance. Provision is made for the licensing authority to maintain a register of permits issued. Permits cannot be issued to vessels or vehicles.

609.   Under *paragraphs 6 to 10*, the authority may prepare a statement of its principles in respect of the issue of these permits, and this can include matters which they propose to take into account in considering the suitability of an applicant. In exercising its functions under Schedule 10, including determining any application, the authority may have regard to the licensing objectives but must have regard to any guidance issued by the Commission. The authority must consult the local police prior to granting an application.

610.   *Paragraph 11* concerns the form and content of permits. Under *paragraphs 12 to 21*, permits will normally last 10 years, but will lapse if the holder ceases to occupy

the premises, dies, becomes unfit to hold the licence or becomes bankrupt or insolvent. The notes relating to prize gaming permits under Part 14 expand upon the meaning of "occupy" for these purposes. Lapsed permits may, however, remain in force for up to six months. This is to allow an orderly transfer of the affairs of the licence holder, and the maintenance of the business (with its machines) while a new permit is obtained. Permits cannot be transferred, but must be re-applied for if there is a new occupier of the premises to which the permit relates.

611.   Holders may surrender their permits voluntarily, and a court may order forfeiture of a permit if the holder is convicted of any relevant offence (see section 126). Permits can be renewed, and a licensing authority may only refuse the application for renewal if access to the FEC by an authorised officer has been refused without reasonable excuse, or renewal would not be reasonably consistent with pursuit of the licensing objectives.

612.   There is an appeal mechanism provided for those who wish to contest a decision of a licensing authority under this Schedule.

Sections 248 & 249: No and limited prizes
613.   Making a gaming machine available for use will be an offence under Part 10, unless the required authorisation, licence or permit is held for the machine. However, in a number of circumstances no offence will be committed where someone makes a gaming machine available for use. These are:

- Where a person using a machine has no opportunity to win a prize, whether or not he pays for use of the machine (section 248). If a prize (as defined in the Act) is available, a machine is a gaming machine, even if there is no payment required to use it;

- Where a person, whether they pay for the machine or not, has the opportunity to win only a limited prize as follows:

  - Solely another opportunity to play the machine (sections 248 and 239); or
  - A prize whose value does not exceed any payment made for use of the machine (section 249).

614.   The sections define payment for use broadly, and this includes payments which entitle someone to use a machine e.g. entrance charges to premises where machines are located. Section 343 contains powers for the Secretary of State to make rules about how to determine the value of a prize.

615.   Power is also provided for the Secretary of State to make regulations which exempt certain gaming machines from the licensing requirements for manufacture, supply, etc. (section 248(2)). This will be where a machine is not designed or expected to be used to provide an opportunity to win a prize. An example of the type of machine which will be included in such regulations is a pin-ball machine, where a

game of chance is offered by the machine, but with no prize, or no more than the possibility of another free go on the machine. In these circumstances there is no regulatory requirement for the machine to be manufactured or supplied under licence. This is a change to the regime under the Gaming Act 1968, where machines continued to require a certificate under section 27 of that Act, even if their subsequent use was not regulated as use of a gaming machine. Machines which offer a limited prize within the meaning of section 249 will require a gaming machine technical operating licence.

Section 250: Single-machine supply and maintenance permits

616.   This section sets out an exception to the general rule that a person who supplies, etc., a gaming machine must hold a gaming machine technical operating licence. It allows the Commission to issue a permit in relation to a specific gaming machine that authorises its supply, repair, installation, or maintenance without an operating licence. A fee is payable for the permit.

617.   The Commission can only grant a single-machine permit if it believes that the supply etc., of the machine will not have any impact on the licensing objectives. This permit procedure replaces the permits issued by the Gaming Board under section 27 of the Gaming Act 1968, to individuals outside the gambling business who have single machines which they wish to dispose of, or repair.

618.   Regulations under section 248(2) could also be used to deal with circumstances where obtaining a permit was considered an onerous obligation for the particular activity concerned, and the gaming machine was not to be used in a manner which permitted it to deliver prizes.

PART 11: LOTTERIES

619.   This Part of the Act makes provision with respect to lotteries, and should be read in conjunction with Schedules 2 and 11. The provisions here are built upon the foundation of the Lotteries and Amusements Act 1976, which will be repealed by this Act on commencement.

620.   The core definition of a lottery is set out in Part 1 of the Act (section 14), as are sections dealing with the overlap between betting, gaming and a lottery.

621.   The promotion of a lottery is unlawful under the Act unless the lottery is of a type that is specifically permitted. There are two permitted types of lottery under the Act:

- lotteries that are run in accordance with an operating licence issued under Part 5; and

- exempt lotteries under Schedule 11. There are four types of exempt lottery set out in Schedule 11.

Section 252: Promoting a lottery

622.   This section clarifies what is meant by the promotion of a lottery. *Subsection (2)* sets out the activities which constitute promoting a lottery. A person promotes a lottery if (amongst other things) he arranges for the printing, distribution or publication of promotional material. *Subsection (3)* defines "promotional material" as a document that advertises, invites participation in, contains information about how to participate in, or lists winners in, a particular lottery.

623.   Where an external lottery manager is retained to carry out the arrangements for a lottery on behalf of a society or local authority, a lottery is regarded, for the purposes of the Act, as being promoted by both the lottery manager and the society or local authority itself.

Section 253: Lottery ticket

624.   This section describes the types of item that may constitute a lottery ticket. It includes any document or article which confers or proves membership of the class eligible for prizes. The definition is deliberately wide so as to include electronic tickets and other items that may not be in the traditional paper format. The terms "sale", "supply" and "purchase" are defined here in relation to lottery tickets. Requirements as to the form and content of a lottery ticket are set out in section 99 (in respect of licensed lotteries) and Schedule 11 (in respect of exempt lotteries).

Sections 254 to 256: Key terms

625.   These sections define certain key terms in relation to lotteries. "Proceeds" is the total amount paid for the tickets in the lottery, before any deductions. "Profits" refers to that amount, less deductions for prizes, sums "rolled over" to another lottery, and reasonable organisational expenses.

626.   Section 255 explains what is meant by the term "draw" in a lottery. The term is defined widely, to include any process by which a prize in a lottery is allocated.

627.   A definition of "rollover" in relation to a lottery is provided in section 256. A rollover occurs when a prize that has not been allocated in one lottery, is added to prizes available for allocation in a subsequent lottery. Where prizes from previous draws are made available in the next draw of the same lottery, this will not be a rollover.

628.   This section also explains where the line is to be drawn between one lottery and another. A lottery may have more than one draw, but multiple draws will only be part of the same lottery where the lottery is arranged in such a way that the class of persons eligible for prizes remains the same. A new lottery will begin where the class of persons eligible for prizes changes, or may change.

Section 257: External lottery manager

629.   The term "external lottery manager" is defined here as a person independent of the society or local authority for whom the lottery is run, who makes the arrangements for the lottery on behalf of the society or local authority. The purpose of this section, when read together with sections 258(3) and 259(3) is to provide that those persons who work with, or on behalf of, societies and local authorities to set up and run the lottery are external lottery managers. Other individuals, who are involved in some ancillary way (for example by selling tickets), are not making arrangements for the lottery and are therefore not external lottery managers. Such individuals do not commit any offence under this Part if they act in accordance with an operating licence held by an external lottery manager or a society or local authority.

Section 258: Promotion of lottery

630.   This section makes it an offence to promote a lottery, but no offence is committed under this section if the person concerned holds and complies with an appropriate operating licence; or the person acts (except as an external lottery manager) on behalf of someone who holds such a licence, and the activity in question is carried on in compliance with that licence. Operating licences can be issued to local authorities, larger non-commercial societies, or to an external lottery manager acting on their behalf (see Part 5 for details of these procedures).

631.   In addition, no offence is committed if the lottery falls into one of the exempt categories set out in Schedule 11. These are:

- incidental non-commercial lotteries;

- private lotteries;

- customer lotteries; and

- small society lotteries (i.e. society lotteries which do not generate sufficient proceeds to require an operating licence from the Commission, and are instead required to be registered with the local authority).

632.   It will be a defence for the person to show that he reasonably believed that he was not committing the offence because:

- the lottery was an exempt lottery under Schedule 11, or a lottery operating licence was held and complied with;

- the arrangement was part of the National Lottery; or

- the arrangement did not fall within the definition of "lottery" under Part 1.

633.   There is a further defence set out in section 265, where a person reasonably believed that the lottery was not one to which this Part applied because it was outside the territorial application of this Part.

Section 259: Facilitating a lottery

634.   This section makes it an offence to facilitate a lottery, which means in this context, advertising a particular lottery, or printing tickets or promotional material for it. Since it is provided that these actions must be with respect to a "particular lottery", this offence is not intended to capture those who, for example, print generic tickets that can be used in lotteries generally.

635.   The offence will not apply if the lottery is exempt, or if a person acts in accordance with the terms and conditions of an operating licence. A person does not need to be a licence holder themselves to benefit from this exemption; they will be covered if they act for the licence holder (for example, if they are an employee, or someone who provides services, such as a printing company).

636.   It will be a defence for the person to show that he reasonably believed that:

- the lottery was an exempt lottery under Schedule 11, or a lottery operating licence was held and complied with;

- the arrangement was part of the National Lottery; or

- the arrangement did not fall within the definition of "lottery" under Part 1.

637.   As with the offence of promoting a lottery, there is a further defence to the offence in this section set out in section 265, where a person reasonably believed that the lottery was not one to which this Part applied because it was outside the territorial application of this Part.

Section 260: Misusing profits of lottery

638.   This section provides for a general offence of misusing the profits of a lottery. A person will commit the offence if the promoter has, in a statement appearing on the lottery tickets or in an advertisement for a lottery ticket, declared that the proceeds of the lottery are to be used for a particular purpose, and the person uses (or permits to be used) all or any of the proceeds for something other than the purpose stated. This offence is not restricted to any particular type of lottery, and can apply to any lottery where such a fund-raising purpose has been declared.

Section 261: Misusing profits of an exempt lottery

639.   This section applies only to certain kinds of exempt lottery (incidental non-commercial lotteries, private society lotteries and small society lotteries), in respect of which there are restrictions on the purposes for which the lottery can be promoted. Under this provision, it will be an offence for a person to use (or permit to be used) any part of the profits of the lottery for a purpose other than a permitted one.

Section 262: Small society lottery: breach of condition

640.   This section provides that a non-commercial society commits an offence if a small society lottery is promoted on its behalf without the necessary registration with the local authority. It is also an offence to fail to comply with the obligation to file a

statement of the matters prescribed in *paragraph 39* of Schedule 11 with the registering authority, or to submit false or misleading information in that statement.

Section 263: Penalty

641.   The maximum penalty upon conviction for any of the offences contained in this Part is a term of imprisonment of up to 51 weeks in England and Wales, or 6 months in Scotland, together with a fine not exceeding level 5 on the standard scale.

Section 264: Exclusion of the National Lottery

642.   This section excludes lotteries that form part of the National Lottery from the provisions of this Part. The National Lottery is regulated under the National Lottery etc. Act 1993 (c.39), but see also Part 1 of this Act.

Section 265: Territorial Application

643.   This section sets out the territorial area over which Part 11 is to apply. It provides that Part 11 applies to anything done in relation to a lottery in Great Britain, or by means of remote gambling equipment in Great Britain. So, if a lottery is provided electronically, and the servers are located in Great Britain, that may be a lottery that falls to be regulated under this Part.

644.   However, the territorial application of Part 11 is limited by this section, so that Part 11 does not regulate any lottery where:

- the only people who become participants in it are outside Great Britain; and

- where there is no-one in Great Britain who possesses tickets with the intention of selling or supplying them to other individuals in Great Britain.

645.   The effect of this is that as soon as a person in Britain becomes a participant in a lottery, or a person possesses tickets with a view to their sale in Great Britain, the lottery will be regulated by Part 11.

646.   This section also provides a defence where a person reasonably believed that no person in Great Britain would become a participant in the lottery; or that there was no intention to sell tickets to people in Great Britain. Without this defence, innocent printers and distributors could be guilty of promoting or facilitating a lottery, even where they had honestly believed that the tickets they were printing or distributing would only be sold abroad.

Schedule 11: Exempt lotteries

647.   This Schedule sets out the requirements that must be complied with in order for a lottery to be classed as "exempt". Exempt lotteries are those that are permitted to be run without an operating licence. There are four types of exempt lottery: incidental non-commercial lotteries, private lotteries, customer lotteries, and small society lotteries.

648. Part 1 of this Schedule deals with incidental non-commercial lotteries; Part 2 with private lotteries; Part 3 with customer lotteries; and Parts 4 and 5 with small society lotteries and their registration with the local authority. Part 6 sets out certain additional powers of the Secretary of State, and Part 7 is interpretative.

Part 1: Incidental non-commercial lotteries
649. This type of lottery replaces those permitted under section 3 (small lotteries incidental to exempt entertainments) and section 15 (provision of amusements with prizes at exempt entertainments) of the Lotteries and Amusements Act 1976 (c.32). An incidental non-commercial lottery is one that is incidental to a non-commercial event, and in respect of which, all the conditions set out in the rest of this Part are complied with. An event is a non-commercial event if the money raised from the event goes entirely to purposes that are not for private gain (*paragraph 2*).

650. The conditions that must be complied with are:

- The promoters of the lottery cannot deduct money from the proceeds of the lottery, for prizes or other costs, in excess of any sums prescribed by the Secretary of State in regulations;

- The lottery must itself be promoted for a purpose other than that of private gain;

- The lottery cannot involve a rollover; and

- Tickets must be sold at the event location during the event, and the result made public while the event is going on.

Part 2: Private Lotteries
651. There are three types of "private lottery" which qualify as exempt lotteries:

- A <u>private society lottery</u>: this must be promoted for, and by, members of a society, although people on the society's premises (as defined in *paragraph 10(1)(b)*) may also purchase tickets. The lottery may be promoted for a purpose for which the society is conducted (*paragraph 13*), and the society can be any group or society, provided it is not established and conducted for purposes connected to gambling;

- A <u>work lottery</u>: this must not make any profit (i.e. all the proceeds must be used for prizes or reasonable costs – see paragraph 13), and must be promoted for and by people working on the same premises (as defined in *paragraph 11(2)*); and

- A <u>residents' lottery</u>: this must not make any profit (i.e. all the proceeds must be used for prizes or reasonable costs), and must be promoted for and by persons who live in a single set of premises (for instance, a hall of residence). The residency requirement can still be satisfied, where the premises are not the sole premises in which a person resides (*paragraph 12(2)*).

652.   All three types of private lottery must comply with the conditions set out in Part 2. These conditions concern:

- Advertising (*paragraph 14*);

- Rollovers (*paragraph 19*); and

- Conditions relating to the price and format of lottery tickets (*paragraphs 15 to 18*).

Part 3: Customer lottery

653.   Under Part 3, a customer lottery is a lottery run by occupiers of business premises, who sell tickets only to customers present on their premises. All the conditions in this Part must be satisfied. These include that:

- the lottery must be arranged to ensure that no profits are made, i.e. the proceeds must be exhausted entirely in the reasonable expenses of the lottery and in the provision of prizes;

- the lottery may only be advertised on the premises on which it is held; and

- no ticket may result in the winner receiving a prize worth more than £50 (the Secretary of State can vary this amount by order, under Part 6 of this Schedule).

654.   Other conditions prohibit rollover, set rules on the frequency with which customer lotteries can be conducted, and make rules relating to lottery tickets.

Parts 4 and 5: Small society lotteries

655.   Under Part 4, a small society lottery is a lottery promoted on behalf of a non-commercial society (as defined in section 19 of the Act), the proceeds of which fall below the thresholds set out in *paragraph 31* of this Part. Such a lottery will be exempt only if all relevant conditions set out in Parts 4 and 5 are complied with.

656.   Small society lotteries are distinguished from large society lotteries by the amount of the proceeds that they generate. A large society lottery requires an operating licence from the Commission under Part 5 of the Act. A lottery is a large society lottery if its proceeds exceed the thresholds set out in paragraph 31.

657.   Where the proceeds fall below these thresholds, the lottery qualifies as a small society lottery, and is regulated by these Parts of Schedule 11. The Secretary of State may change these thresholds in regulations.

658.   A small society lottery may be promoted for any of the purposes of the society (*paragraph 32*). As with large society lotteries, at least 20% of the proceeds must go to a purpose for which the society is conducted (*paragraph 33*). No single prize may

be worth more than the amount set out in paragraph 34. Small society lotteries may have rollovers, although rollovers are only permitted where every lottery that may be affected by the rollover is also a small society lottery and the rollover will not permit any person to win more than the amount in paragraph 34 (*paragraphs 34 and 35*). This amount may be varied by the Secretary of State in regulations under Part 6.

659.   Conditions are also set out in *paragraphs 36 and 37* relating to the format and price of tickets. As is the case for large society lotteries, one document can be a ticket for the purpose of entering a number of lotteries, so long as the dates of the draw in those lotteries can be ascertained from the information on the ticket. Tickets for small society lotteries need not be paper documents – they may also be electronic. If a ticket is an electronic ticket, however, it must be capable of being printed, or stored electronically.

660.   A society must be registered with a local authority (in England and Wales) or licensing board (in Scotland), in accordance with Part 5 of the Schedule while any small society lottery is being promoted.

661.   The society must send to the local authority with which it is registered, a statement of the matters listed in *paragraph 39(2)*. This includes information as to:

- The arrangements for the lottery (dates, prizes, proceeds etc.);
- Amounts deducted by the promoters for prizes and costs;
- Whether any other costs were paid, other than from the proceeds of the lottery.

662.   Two members of the society, or its governing body, must sign a statement sent to the local authority. If a local authority receives a statement, and they think that the lottery was, in fact, a large lottery, they must notify the Commission.

663.   The provisions for registration, in Part 5, set out the mechanisms for application, registration, refusal, revocation, cancellation and appeal against decisions made in relation to the registration of a small society lottery. Appeal is to the Magistrates Court and, in Scotland, to the Sheriff. There is an annual registration fee of an amount to be prescribed by the Secretary of State and Scottish Ministers in regulations. Local authorities and licensing boards must keep a register of all societies registered under this Part, and must notify the Commission when they register any society.

Part 6: Powers to impose additional restrictions
664.   Part 6 sets out the powers for the Secretary of State to impose additional restrictions, by regulations, on the exempt lotteries described in this Part:

- requiring that tickets are distributed by hand rather than post; and
- relating to the use of rollover   arrangements.

665.   This Part also gives the Secretary of State the power to make orders relating to classes of lottery with the following effect:

- imposing further conditions on exempt lotteries (in particular in relation to those matters listed in paragraph *59(2)*);

- restricting the extent to which a person can rely on the exemptions set out in Schedule 11. Such an order may, in particular, further restrict the number of exempt lotteries that may be promoted in any period or the minimum interval between two exempt lotteries promoted on behalf of any person.

666.   Before exercising these powers, the Secretary of State must consult the Commission.

667.   The Secretary of State may also, by order, vary a monetary amount or a percentage set out in this Schedule.

Part 7: General

668.   Part 7 explains terms and phrases used in Schedule 11. It also clarifies that, other than in respect of private lotteries or customer lotteries, the provisions of the Schedule apply to activities on a vessel.

PART 12: CLUBS, PUBS, FAIRS, &C.

669.   This Part provides certain gaming allowances, and additional authorisation procedures for gaming and gaming machines for:

- Members' clubs;

- Commercial clubs;

- Miners' welfare institutes;

- Alcohol licensed premises; and

- Travelling fairs.

670.   Under the Gaming Act 1968 these various associations, premises and entities are afforded particular gaming entitlements, either as of right, or with express permission. Once commenced, this Act repeals those provisions of the 1968 Act, and this Part provides a replacement regime. This Part does not provide any entitlements to conduct betting or lotteries, only gaming and the use of gaming machines.

671.   Part 10 of the Act contains power for the categorisation of gaming machines, which is relevant to this Part. Part 18 of the Act contains sections which make provision for determining the value of a prize, and defining participation fee and stake.

672. Where a reference is made in this Part to a Commission code of practice, it means a statutory code of practice, issued under the Commission's powers in Part 2 of the Act.

673. This Part contains powers for Scottish Ministers to make regulations about the procedural requirements for club gaming permits and club gaming machine permits and licensed premises gaming machine permits in Scotland.

Sections 266 to 268: Definitions of eligible clubs

674. There are three categories of eligible club: members' clubs, commercial clubs and miners' welfare institutes. To take advantage of the various gaming rights in Part 12 a club has to bring itself within one of these categories (although not all gaming rights are equally available to all three categories of club).

675. **Members' clubs** must have at least 25 members and be established and conducted wholly or mainly for purposes other than gaming (unless the gaming is of a prescribed kind). They are to be established and conducted for the benefit of their members. They are also to be established with the intention of operating on an ongoing basis, and not temporarily. Examples of such clubs would include local political associations, working men's clubs or branches of the Royal British Legion.

676. *Subsection (2)* permits the Secretary of State to prescribe particular kinds of gaming. It is proposed that bridge and whist be so prescribed. This allows members' clubs established for the purposes of providing such gaming to take advantage of rights under Part 12, notwithstanding the restriction in subsection (1)(a). This maintains the position under the Gaming Act 1968. See also the provision for exempt gaming under section 269(1)(c).

677. **Commercial clubs** are subject to the same conditions as members' clubs, except that members' clubs must not operate as a commercial enterprise which benefits a class of people different to the members. Commercial clubs, on the other hand, can. These clubs can also be known as proprietary clubs. An example of a commercial club would be a snooker club. Like members' clubs, commercial clubs may also be gaming clubs, provided the gaming is of a type prescribed in regulations under *subsection (2)*, although this proviso does not apply to exempt gaming under section 269.

678. The definition of **miners' welfare institutes** has been amended from that contained in the Gaming Act 1968. Under Part 12 miners' welfare institutes are associations established for social or recreational purposes, where the association is either managed by a group of miners' representatives or uses premises regulated under a charitable trust, where the trust has, at some time, received funds from one of a number of mining related organisations. The definition of "miners' representative" has been revised to take account of changes in mining communities and ex-mining communities. Furthermore, the alternative limb for qualification as a miners' welfare institute has been amended to allow for the broader social aims that institutes in ex-

mining areas now promote. The definition in section 268 replaces that in the Gaming Act 1968.

Sections 269 & 270: Exempt gaming

679.   This section permits members' clubs, commercial clubs and miners' welfare institutes to provide certain facilities for gaming without the need for any express authorisation. In order to qualify for this exemption the gaming must meet a number of conditions:

- It must be equal chance gaming, as defined in Part 1 of the Act;

- Stakes and prizes must be in accordance with any rules or limits prescribed in regulations;

- The club must not deduct any amounts from sums staked or won in the gaming;

- Any charge for participation (which is broadly defined) must not exceed amounts prescribed in regulations (and see section 344);

- The games played may only take place on one set of premises meaning there may not be any linking of games between premises; and

- People may only participate in the gaming if they have been a member of the club (or applied or were nominated for membership) at least 48 hours before playing, or are the genuine guests of such a person (but this does not apply to commercial clubs).

680.   These conditions are similar to those set out in section 40 of the 1968 Act, which the Act repeals, with the exception of the restriction on linking games and the addition of a power to prescribe maximum stakes and prizes, which are new. The gaming allowances under section 269 may be used by any members' or commercial club that is permanent and has at least 25 members, even if it is established for gaming. There is no requirement for the gaming to be of a prescribed kind (see section 269(1)(c) and (d)).

681.   Under section 270, subsections (2) and (4), different requirements about the limits on stakes, prizes, and participation fees may be set for different types of club or institute, for different types of game, and for different types of fee.

Sections 271 & 272: Club gaming permit

682.   Members' clubs (but not commercial clubs) and miners' welfare institutes may apply for a club gaming permit from a licensing authority to authorise the provision of games of chance and gaming machines on premises from which the club operates. This permit allows clubs and institutes to offer gaming facilities, in addition to those available under the exempt gaming allowances. Schedule 12 sets out the procedure and rules for this permit.

683.   The club gaming permit will authorise the provision of up to 3 gaming

machines in categories B, C or D (but no more than 3 machines in total). The permit is subject to the condition that no person under 18 shall use a Category B or C machine, and the holder of the permit must comply with a Commission code of practice about the location and operation of gaming machines.

684.   The club gaming permit will also authorise additional gaming facilities to be provided. This gaming falls into two types:

- Equal chance gaming. This is equivalent to that authorised under the exempt gaming allowances in sections 269 and 270, but without any prescribed limits on maximum stakes or prizes. The other conditions set for exempt gaming apply equally to this entitlement; and

- Such games of chance as are prescribed in regulations. This provision allows the Secretary of State to authorise particular games involving a bank or unequal chance games to be played under the permit. Under the Gaming Act 1968 pontoon and chemin de fer were permitted. This gaming is subject to a number of conditions set out in section 217(4), and also rules which the Secretary of State may prescribe.

685.   The Secretary of State may make regulations which set different maximum participation fees for exempt gaming and gaming authorised by a club gaming permit. By this means a club which holds a club gaming permit can be permitted to make different charges for equal chance gaming, to a club which relies solely on the exempt gaming provisions in section 269.

Section 273: Club machine permit
686.   Under this section a club machine permit is available to a members' club, miners' welfare institute or a commercial club. This type of permit authorises the holder to provide up to 3 gaming machines in Category B, C or D (but no more than 3 machines in total) on premises from which the club operates. It does not authorise the provision of any other type of facilities for gaming. Three conditions are automatically attached to a club machine permit. These relate to prior membership for use of the machines (but not for a commercial club), restrictions on giving children and young people access to Category C or B machines; and requiring compliance with Commission codes of practice about the location and operation of machines.

687.   Schedule 12 sets out the procedure in relation to an application for a club machine permit, and the rules which apply to its maintenance and validity.

Section 274: Procedure
688.   Schedule 12 contains the detailed rules for the two types of club permit, in relation to England and Wales. In relation to Scotland, different procedures to those in Schedule 12 will apply if Scottish Ministers exercise their powers under section 285. These powers enable different procedural rules to be set for clubs or institutes holding a certificate of registration under the Licensing (Scotland) Act 1976, or for clubs or

institutes of such other type as may be specified in the regulations.

Schedule 12: Club gaming permits and club machine permits

689.   Schedule 12 contains the procedures for obtaining club gaming and club machine permits, and the rules for their duration, maintenance, renewal and cancellation. Licensing authorities will issue both types of permit, and must keep registers of permits granted.

690.   By virtue of *paragraphs 27 and 28* a licensing authority must have regard to Commission guidance and the licensing objectives in undertaking its functions under this Schedule.

691.   *Paragraphs 1 to 9* include a requirement that applications for a permit are copied to the Commission and the police, who may object to the application, in which case a hearing will be required, unless all the parties agree otherwise.

692.   Under *paragraph 6* the licensing authority may only refuse an application on certain grounds. These grounds are that:

- The applicant does not fulfil the requirements for a members' or commercial club or miners' welfare institute and therefore is not entitled to receive the type of permit for which it has applied;

- The applicant's premises are used wholly or mainly by children or young people;

- An offence under the Act or a breach of a permit has been committed by the applicant while providing gaming facilities;

- A permit held by the applicant has been cancelled in the previous 10 years; or

- An objection has been lodged by the Commission or the police.

693.   If the authority is satisfied that (a) or (b) are the case it must refuse the application. If (c), (d) or (e) is at issue the licensing authority may reject the licence if they think fit, taking account of any relevant guidance issued by the Commission and the licensing objectives.

694.   A licensing authority has no discretion to attach conditions to a club machine permit or club gaming permit. Part 12 of the Act sets out particular conditions which are to apply universally to permits of either type.

695.   *Paragraph 10* provides a fast track procedure for clubs or institutes in England and Wales which hold a club premises certificate under section 72 of the Licensing Act 2003 (authorising the sale or supply of alcohol or provision of regulated entertainment). Under the fast-track procedure there is no opportunity for objections to be made by the Commission or the police, and the grounds upon which an authority can refuse a permit are reduced. This is because the club or institute will already have

been through a licensing process in relation to its club premises certificate under the 2003 Act, and to impose the full requirements of Schedule 12 would produce unwarranted duplication and cost. This fast track procedure does not apply in Scotland. Instead, Scottish Ministers can make alternative provision using their powers under section 285.

696.   *Paragraph 11* deals with the form and content of permits, and *paragraphs 12 to 16* with their maintenance, including variation of permits if the information in them becomes inaccurate. *Paragraphs 17 to 20* provide that permits, with one exception, will last for ten years (in which case they can be renewed) unless they cease to have effect under another provision of the Schedule. These provisions are those for: lapse, surrender, cancellation and forfeiture.

697.   The exception to the ten year duration is that where a permit has been granted under the fast track procedure under paragraph 10, such permits last indefinitely unless the club premises certificate under the Licensing Act 2003 ceases to have effect, or is surrendered, cancelled, or forfeited.

698.   *Paragraph 25* sets out full appeal rights from the decisions of licensing authorities under this Schedule.

Sections 275 & 281: Bingo in clubs and alcohol licensed premises

699.   These sections contain particular provisions regulating bingo played pursuant to any of the authorisations in this Part by clubs or miners' welfare institutes, or on alcohol licensed premises. The purpose of sections 275 and 281 is to prevent facilities for bingo being offered on a large scale (high turnover bingo) under the various authorisations in this Part. Where a club, miners' welfare institute, or alcohol licensed premises wishes to offer high turnover bingo it will require a bingo operating licence from the Commission, under Part 5. In such cases, clubs and miners' welfare institutes are relieved from the general obligation under Part 5 to have at least one management office in the organisation held by a personal licence holder, under section 80(9).

700.   The trigger for needing a bingo operating licence is that "high turnover bingo" is played in a "high turnover period", and sections 275 and 281 provide identical and comprehensive definitions for both terms. The key element is that the total stakes or prizes for bingo games played in any period for 7 days exceed £2000. Subject to appropriate Parliamentary approval, this figure can be amended by the Secretary of State by order.

701.   If a club or institute plays high turnover bingo without the appropriate operating licence it will commit an offence under section 33. Sections 275 and 281 operate in a way which means that offences are only committed after a club or institute has had its first week of high turnover bingo. Once that has happened an offence takes place if high turnover bingo is played again in the following 12 month period, unless a bingo operating licence has been obtained. In addition, a club or

institute must inform the Commission whenever a high turnover period first begins (i.e. when it has had its first week of high turnover bingo), and failure to so is an offence, with a maximum penalty of a level 3 fine.

Sections 277 & 278: Alcohol licensed premises

702. Sections 279 to 284 are concerned with the provision of gaming, and the making available of gaming machines, in certain premises which are licensed to supply alcohol for consumption on the premises under Part 3 of the Licensing Act 2003 or under section 9(1) of the Licensing (Scotland) Act 1976.

703. The relevant premises are those which contain a bar at which alcohol is served for consumption on the premises. This means that premises such as restaurants which do not have a bar for serving drinks to customers will fall outside the scope of the premises to which sections 279 to 284 apply. The sections also do not apply to vehicles.

704. The gaming and gaming machine exemptions conferred by sections 279 to 284 only apply at those times when alcohol is authorised to be sold at the premises.

705. A reference to "alcohol licensed premises" in these notes means premises which are within the scope of sections 277 and 278.

Sections 279 & 280: Exempt gaming

706. This section authorises the provision of gaming facilities on alcohol licensed premises, provided the gaming complies with certain conditions. No further authorisation is required to make the gaming lawful, provided the conditions are complied with.

707. The conditions are as follows:

- The facilities are limited to equal chance gaming;

- Stakes and prizes for the gaming must not exceed any limits as to value or amount prescribed by the Secretary of State;

- No amount may be deducted or levied from amounts staked or won;

- No participation fees may be charged (and this includes membership subscriptions, see section 344(3));

- The games played may only take place on one set of alcohol-licensed premises, i.e. there may not be any linking of games between premises; and

- Children and young people must be excluded from the gaming.

708. Under section 6 of the Gaming Act 1968 (general provisions as to gaming on premises licensed for retail sale of liquor) cribbage and dominoes may be played for winnings at premises licensed to sell alcohol for consumption on the premises. It is also possible, under section 6, for the holder of such a licence to apply for permission

for other forms of gaming on the premises. In all cases conditions may be made to prevent high-stake gaming taking place, and to ensure the gaming does not become the main inducement to attend the premises. The Act repeals this section, and sections 279 and 280 contain the replacement provisions.

Section 282: Gaming machines: automatic entitlement

709.   This section authorises up to 2 Category C or D gaming machines to be made available on alcohol licensed premises. It does this by exempting such premises from the premises offence in Part 3 (section 37) and the offence relating to making gaming machines available in Part 10 (section 242). This exemption only applies if the person who holds the relevant alcohol licence has notified the licensing authority of his intention to make gaming machines available, and has paid the required notification fee. The section is also subject to the condition that gaming machines are to be made available in compliance with any relevant provision of a code of practice issued by the Gambling Commission.

710.   This section, together with the other provisions of this Part on gaming machines in alcohol licensed premises, replace the provisions of section 34 of, and Schedule 9 to, the Gaming Act 1968 for the grant of permits to alcohol licensed premises.

Section 283: Licensed premises gaming machine permits

711.   This section allows further Category C or D gaming machines to be made available in alcohol licensed premises (in addition to the two machines authorised under section 282) in accordance with a permit known as a licensed premises gaming machine permit. No limit is imposed on the number of gaming machines that can be made available under this section. The permit will provide in each case for the number of Category C or D gaming machines that it authorises.

Schedule 13: Licensed premises gaming machine permits

712.   This Schedule makes further provision with respect to licensed premises gaming machine permits. This Schedule does not have effect in relation to Scotland. Section 285 enables Scottish Ministers to make provision by regulations in respect of licensed premises gaming machine permits which is to have effect in place of that in Schedule 13.

713.   *Paragraphs 1 to 6* set out the process for making applications for such a permit. By virtue of paragraph 5, a licensing authority may not attach conditions to a permit. Under paragraph 6, a licensing authority may not refuse an application or grant a permit for a different category or a smaller number of gaming machines unless they have notified the applicant and given him the opportunity to make representations.

714.   There is no limit on the duration of a permit. *Paragraph 12* provides for it to continue unless and until it ceases to have effect under a provision of the Schedule.

715.   *Paragraph 16* enables the licensing authority to cancel or vary the permit. The authority may only take such action in the circumstances specified in sub-paragraph (1), namely if-

- it would not be reasonably consistent with pursuit of the licensing objectives for the permit to continue to have effect;

- gaming has taken place on the premises in breach of the permit or a condition of the permit;

- the premises are mainly used for making gaming machines available; or

- an offence under the Act has been committed on the premises.

716.   The licensing authority is required, before cancelling or varying a permit, to give the permit holder at least 21 days' notice and to consider any representations made by the permit holder. The authority is required to hold a hearing if the permit holder requests one.

717.   *Paragraphs 19 and 20* make provision for transfer of permits. *Paragraph 21* sets out rights of appeal.

718.   *Paragraph 22* requires the licensing authority to maintain a register of permits. The Secretary of State may make regulations about how the licensing authority record and use this information.

Section 284: Removal of exemption
719.   This section enables the licensing authority to make an order in respect of specific premises, removing the right to provide exempt gaming at those premises under section 279 or the right to make up to 2 gaming machines available for use in accordance with section 282.

720.   The licensing authority may only make an order under this section if-

- it would not be reasonably consistent with pursuit of the licensing objectives for the exemption or entitlement conferred by the relevant section to continue to have effect;

- gaming has taken place on the premises in reliance on the exemption or entitlement conferred by the relevant section, but in breach of a condition of that section. An example of such a breach would be where gaming machines were made available in breach of a relevant code of practice issued by the Gambling Commission;

- the premises are mainly used for gaming; or

- an offence under the Act has been committed on the premises.

721.   Before making an order under this section, the licensing authority must give

21 days' notice to the holder of the alcohol licence, allow representations to be made, and hold a hearing if the licensee requests one. The licensee also has a right to appeal to a magistrates' court (or sheriff's court in Scotland) against any decision of the licensing authority under this section.

Section 285: Permits for clubs, pubs etc.: special provision for Scotland

722.   This section enables Scottish Ministers, with the consent of the Secretary of State, to make provision by regulations in respect of club gaming and machine permits in place of that in Schedule 12, and in respect of licensed premises gaming machine permits in place of that in Schedule 13.

Sections 286 & 287: Travelling fairs

723.   These sections:

- define a "travelling fair" for the purposes of the Act, and

- grant travelling fairs the right to provide unlimited numbers of Category D gaming machines, provided any facilities for gambling offered at the fair are no more than an ancillary amusement.

724.   Fairs are also entitled to offer equal chance prize gaming, under Part 13 of the Act. This means that any prize gaming and any gaming machines made available must not be the principal activities at the fair. Instead, in order to offer these limited gambling facilities, the fair must be composed mainly of non-gambling amusements and activities.

PART 13: PRIZE GAMING

725.   Part 13 contains authorisations for prize gaming. This is a type of gaming where the organiser puts up the prizes in advance, as distinct from gaming where the stakes of the participants make up the winnings. Prize gaming is intended to permit low level gaming, for small participation fees, and modest prizes. Bingo played at seaside amusement arcades is a typical venue for such gaming.

726.   The definition of "gaming" in Part 1 covers any sort of gaming for prizes or winnings. Therefore, a provision in the Act which authorises gaming generally, also authorises prize gaming. For example, a bingo operating licence authorises the playing of games of bingo for prizes or winnings. However, in this Part the permissions relate exclusively to prize gaming.

727.   The premises which can receive authorisations under this Part are: adult gaming centres, licensed or unlicensed family entertainment centres, and travelling fairs. There is also a permit for authorising other premises to provide prize gaming, under Schedule 14, and particular allowances for bingo operators.

728.   This   Part   is   derived   from provisions in section 16 (provisions of

amusements with prizes at certain commercial entertainments) of the Lotteries and Amusements Act 1976 (which is repealed by this Act) and section 21 (special provisions as to gaming for prizes) of the Gaming Act 1968 (which is repealed by this Act). This Part does not replicate every aspect of those sections. In particular, lotteries may not be promoted under this Part.

729.   Where machines are used for playing prize games, these may or may not count as gaming machines. This will depend on whether the machine complies with the exemptions in section 235(2)(e), (f) or (g). If it does, it will not be subject to the Part 10 gaming machine regime, but will be subject to regulation by this Part, together with relevant licence conditions and codes of practice. If it does not, it will be a gaming machine, and that regime will apply.

Section 288: Meaning of "prize gaming"

730.   To be prize gaming, the prize for which the gaming is played must comply with the following requirements:

- the nature or size of the prize must not be determined by reference to the number of people playing the game; and

- the nature or size of the prize must not be determined by reference to the amount paid for or raised by the gaming.

731.   This gaming is therefore different to gaming where the stakes paid by the players are used to calculate the winnings available. The effect of the definition is that in prize gaming the prizes available will be determined by the operator of the gaming before play commences, and the payments he receives from the players will not be put directly to any prize on offer. This does not stop operators from estimating what money will be raised from gaming, or predicting the numbers who will take part. Its purpose is to stop the actual amounts raised in a particular game being used to determine the prize in that particular game. Prize gaming can cover both money and non-money prizes.

732.   Section 288 does not prevent prizes being won in a way that depends on the progress or outcome of the game. This means that if different prizes can be claimed dependent on how quickly a win takes place (for example, calling "house" in a game of bingo within a certain number of calls), this is permitted.

Section 289: Prize gaming permits and Schedule 14

733.   One way of authorising prize gaming is to obtain a prize gaming permit from a licensing authority. This section and Schedule 14 make provision for the grant and maintenance of prize gaming permits. Anyone who occupies, or proposes to occupy, premises may apply for a permit, but a permit is not available in respect of premises which are subject to a premises licence under Part 8, or a club gaming permit under Part 12. This is because those licences and permits already give such premises the relevant rights to offer prize gaming, where appropriate. A permit cannot be granted

for a vessel or a vehicle.

734.   The reference to "occupy" in this context means a legal right to be in occupation of the premises. This can either be by having a freehold or leasehold interest in the property, or holding it on a tenancy agreement. A person who is seeking a prize gaming permit must have a right to occupy the premises where the prize gaming takes place. For example, if "A" has a prize gaming permit and owns the freehold of the premises where the prize gaming is taking place, and leases the property to "B", then (subject to the terms of the lease), A will no longer have the right to be in occupation of the premises. On this basis, the permit shall lapse in accordance with *paragraph 14* of Schedule 14. If "B" wishes to offer prize gaming at the premises then he will need to make an application for a new permit under paragraph 3. In these circumstances, "B's" permit will not take effect until the lease has formally been executed in his favour (see paragraph 14(2)).

735.   By virtue of the provisions of Part 4 of the Act, children and young people may only participate in equal chance prize gaming, and not any other form of prize gaming made available pursuant to a permit.   There are a number of conditions applicable to prize gaming permits, which are common to all prize gaming authorised by this Part, contained in section 293.

736.   *Schedule 14* covers the process and procedure of the grant and maintenance of a prize gaming permit. The requirements are similar, but not identical, to those applicable to family entertainment centre gaming machine permits under Part 10 of and Schedule 12 to the Act. The licensing authority must maintain a register of prize gaming permits.

737.   Under *paragraph 8* of *Schedule 14* a licensing authority can prepare a statement of principles which they propose to use for determining applications for permits, and, in particular, the suitability of an applicant. In exercising their functions in relation to prize gaming permits, a licensing authority may have regard to the licensing objectives set out in Part 1 of the Act, but must have regard to any relevant guidance issued by the Commission (paragraph 8(3)). Subject to this, an authority has discretion whether to grant or refuse a permit. *Paragraph 10* requires the authority to consult the police prior to issuing a permit.

738.   Under *paragraphs 13 to 17*, a permit will expire after ten years (when it can be renewed) unless it lapses (in which case certain transitional provisions are made), is surrendered or is forfeited under the provisions of these paragraphs.   Renewal applications are considered on the same grounds as an original application (this is different to the renewal of a family entertainment centre gaming machine permit under *Schedule 12*, where the grounds for refusing renewal are more narrowly defined).   Forfeiture can be ordered by any court sentencing a permit holder for a relevant offence, as defined in section 126.

739.   *Paragraph 22* provides a full appeals procedure for anyone wishing to appeal

against the decisions of a licensing authority under this Schedule.

Sections 290 & 292: Prize gaming in gaming and entertainment centres and fairs

740.   As a separate authorisation to the prize gaming permit, these sections grant rights to conduct prize gaming to licensed adult gaming centres (AGCs), licensed and unlicensed family entertainment premises (FECs), and to travelling fairs. Licensed AGCs and FECs may offer any type of prize gaming, but an unlicensed FEC (i.e. one with a permit under Schedule 10 to the Act), and a travelling fair, may only offer equal chance prize gaming.

741.   The prize gaming which can be offered under these sections is subject to conditions under section 293. In addition, under Part 4 of the Act, children and young people can only participate in equal chance gaming at a licensed or unlicensed FEC or travelling fair. Therefore, if a licensed FEC chooses to offer unequal chance prize gaming, children and young people may not participate in it (people under 18 are not allowed into AGCs at all).

742.   In addition, for prize gaming to be offered lawfully at a fair, the prize gaming, together with any other facilities for gambling offered (e.g. gaming machines), must be ancillary to the other amusements and activities offered at the fair.

Section 291: Bingo halls

743.   Under a bingo operating licence, any form of bingo may be offered. This means prize bingo and cash bingo, as developed under the Gaming Act 1968, are both permitted by the bingo operating licence. However, section 21 of the 1968 Act conferred certain entitlements to offer gaming for prizes upon premises licensed under Part II of that Act, which are not covered entirely by the terms of the bingo operating licence.

744.   Section 291 permits holders of a bingo premises licence (and necessarily a bingo operating licence) to offer prize gaming, provided the gaming complies with any conditions attached to the relevant bingo operating licence. Such conditions may be added as general conditions by the Commission or imposed by the Secretary of State (see the notes on Part 5 for an explanation of these). In particular, the conditions may restrict the types of games offered under this authorisation. Conditions imposed by the Secretary of State may also relate to any of the matters set out in section 91(1) e.g. impose limits on the size of payments made by players to participate in the gaming, or on the size of prizes.

745.   Under the terms of Part 1 and Part 5 of the Act, casinos are granted permission to offer any form of gaming (subject to conditions which may be imposed on a casino operating licence), and no longer need any express permission similar to that offered by section 21 of the 1968 Act. Therefore, Part 13 does not cover casinos.

Section 293: Conditions for prize gaming

746.   There are four conditions that prize gaming permit holders, licensed AGCs,

licensed FECs, FECs with permits and fairs must comply with in order for them to offer prize gaming lawfully under this Part:

- The amounts charged to players to take part in the prize gaming must not exceed any amounts prescribed by the Secretary of State, and these may differ according to different matters (and see section 344 for the definition of participation fee);

- The prizes offered in the prize gaming must not exceed any value set by the Secretary of State (and this may cover money and/or non-money prizes). The limits may be set by reference to each prize that is offered in a game or all the prizes that are offered in a game;

- The prize gaming must take place on the relevant premises, in the course of one day only, and the results must be announced on the premises, and as soon as possible after the game ends; and

- Participation in a game must not entitle the player to participate in any other gambling. In other words, the prize gaming must be free-standing and self-contained, and not linked with other gambling.

Section 294: Power to restrict exemptions
747. This section gives the Secretary of State the power to remove some, or all, of the prize gaming entitlements conferred in this Part. The purpose of this section is to provide flexibility in the event that, for example, an additional class of operating licence is added to Part 5 of the Act which covers matters dealt with under the prize gaming sections. If this were to happen, it would be necessary to remove the entitlements from Part 13, in order for new operating licence requirements to apply. This power is included to deal with such future contingencies.

PART 14: PRIVATE AND NON-COMMERCIAL GAMING AND BETTING

748. This Part provides authorisations for gambling to take place in private, or on non-commercial terms. In particular, it permits various forms of domestic gambling, and also provides authorisations for gaming to take place at non-commercial events.

749. These sections replace various provisions of the Betting, Gaming and Lotteries Act 1963, the Gaming Act 1968, and the Lotteries and Amusements Act 1976. In particular, this Part replaces section 41 (gaming at entertainments not held for private gain) of the 1968 Act and section 15 (provision of amusements with prizes at exempt entertainments) of the 1976 Act. This Part does not provide any authority for the promotion of lotteries. Those elements of the 1976 Act which dealt with lotteries at exempt entertainments (specifically sections 3 and 15) are now dealt with under Part 11 and Schedule 11. The "incidental non-commercial lottery" is the new type of exempt lottery, for what were lotteries at exempt entertainments.

Sections 295 & 296: Private betting and gaming

750.   These sections enable people to participate in and offer facilities for betting and gaming, including on premises, without committing any offence under the Act, provided their activity meets the various conditions for private gaming and betting. Schedule 15 sets out the various conditions.

751.   In addition, these sections contain protection for people who bet, but who are not doing so in the course of a business. The definitions set out in Part 1 of the Act mean that both parties to a bet (sometimes known as the "backer" and the "layer") are capable of providing facilities for betting. This means that, ordinarily, anyone who offers a bet, or accepts a bet will be committing an offence under Part 3, unless he has authorisation under the Act.

752.   Where a person is offering or negotiating bets in the course of a business, (commonly known as "bookmaking"), he will require a betting operating licence under Part 5. Similarly, if someone is using betting as a way of earning a living, so that it renders it a business activity, that too may require a licence. However, there is no regulatory requirement for people who use the services of a betting operator on a non-commercial basis to obtain a licence. Nor should private bets, i.e. between friends, require any form of express authorisation. These sections make it clear that a person does not commit any offence under the Act if he makes or accepts a bet, or offers to do so, provided he is acting in a personal capacity, and not in the course of business.

753.   These provisions apply equally to those using the services of a betting intermediary i.e. an internet betting exchange. The intermediary will require an operating licence under Part 5, but the users of the exchange will benefit from the exemption in these sections, provided their use is in a non-business capacity.

Schedule 15: Private gaming and betting
Part 1: Gaming
754.   Part 1 of the Schedule defines what private gaming constitutes for the purposes of the Act, and identifies two sub-sets of private gaming: domestic gaming and residential gaming.

755.   Gaming is private gaming when:

- it is equal chance gaming;

- no charge is made for participation; and

- the gaming is conducted entirely in private (i.e. in a place to which the public do not have access).

756.   However, where private gaming meets the conditions for domestic or residential gaming, then there is no need for this to be equal chance gaming, and therefore bankers' games and games of unequal chance may be played in these

127

situations.

Part 2: Betting

757.   There are two types of private betting: domestic betting and workplace betting.

Sections 297 to 301: Non-commercial gaming

758.   These sections authorise certain types of gaming to be provided at non-commercial events. A non-commercial event is an event where the money raised from the event is not used for private gain e.g. it is for used for charitable or other generally beneficial purposes. Section 19, by virtue of section 353(1), provides a definition of private gain for these purposes.

759.   These sections require that both money raised from the non-commercial event, and the profits made from the gaming itself, are not used for private gain. This means that if someone other than the organiser of the event provides the facilities for gaming, they too must ensure that the profits go to good causes.

760.   The gaming permitted by these sections is prize gaming (as defined in section 288) and equal chance gaming which complies with a number of conditions:

- All players must be told what purpose the money raised from the gaming is going to be used for (this must be something other than private gain), and the profits must be applied to that purpose;

- The non-commercial event cannot take place on premises with a premises licence (under Part 8) or a temporary use notice (under Part 9). There is nothing to stop such premises running charitable or other gambling events to raise money for good causes, but they should do so using the gambling permissions granted to them by their premises licence or use notice. They cannot rely upon any of the allowances granted in Part 14. The one exception to this is that a non-commercial event can take place at a track licensed under Part 8, and rely upon the allowances in Part 14, provided no licensed activities are taking place at the time. This permits the use of tracks for non-commercial gambling on when races are not taking place.

- The gaming (whether prize or equal chance) cannot be remote gaming. These permissions are only intended to be used at events, on premises, and for gaming in person.

- If the gaming is equal chance gaming, then the gaming must comply with any regulations made by the Secretary of State setting limits on:

    - The stakes, fees or charges for the gaming; and
    - The amount or value of any prize available.

- There are no limits on the fees, charges or value of prizes for prize gaming at a non-commercial event.

761.   In all cases the money raised from the gaming must be used for the fund-

raising purpose specified at the event, and if someone uses any profits from the gaming for something else, then they commit an offence under section 301. The maximum penalty, upon conviction for an offence, is a term of imprisonment not exceeding 51 weeks for England and Wales (six months in Scotland), and/or a level 5 fine.

Section 302: Non-commercial betting

762. This section provides a definition for non-commercial betting. This is betting where neither party is acting in the course of business.

PART 15: INSPECTION

763. Part 15 deals with the powers of entry to and inspection of premises. It sets out the different kinds of inspection and the people who may carry them out, the powers available to such people. both in relation to the circumstances of entry, and activity once on the premises, and the offences for non-compliance with the provisions of this Part. The provisions contain safeguards to ensure that any invasion of privacy is minimised and is proportionate to the purpose for which entry is made. For example, it will not be possible to enter a dwelling under this Part for any reason without a judicial warrant.

Section 303: Enforcement officers

764. The Commission will have power to appoint enforcement officers whose powers are set out in this Part. Enforcement officers may be, but need not be, employees of the Commission.

Section 304: Authorised persons

765. This section makes provision for persons to be "authorised persons" for the purposes of the Act. Authorised persons are given various powers and functions under the Act in relation to inspection of premises in particular when someone is applying for a premises licence. Designated officers of licensing authorities and officers of other authorities who are authorised to exercise certain statutory functions in a particular area are "authorised persons" in relation to premises wholly or partly situated within that area. *Subsection (4)* provides for certain people to be "authorised persons" in relation to any premises wherever situated.

766. An "authorised local authority officer" is a person designated as such by a licensing authority for a purpose relating to premises within the area of the licensing authority.

Section 305: Compliance

767. This section confers express powers on constables, authorised persons and enforcement officers to undertake activities to assess whether a provision of the Act is being complied with or whether an offence is being committed. This provision is connected to section 64. That section provides for the actions of a constable,

enforcement officer or authorised person (or those of a child or young person acting at his request) not to be unlawful under Part 4 if done in performance of his functions under the Act.

Section 306: Suspected offence

768.   Under this section a constable or enforcement officer may enter premises if it is reasonably suspected that an offence under this Act has been, is being or is about to be committed on the premises. Where it is suspected that the offence is being or is about to be committed entry can be made without a warrant (unless the premises is a dwelling).   In cases regarding the past commission of an offence, a constable or enforcement officer may only enter the premises under the authority of a judicial warrant.   An application must be made to a justice of the peace or the sheriff in Scotland to issue a warrant to enter the premises. A warrant can only be issued where the justice of the peace or sheriff is satisfied there are reasonable grounds for suspecting that an offence has been committed and that evidence of the offence may be found on the premises. The justice of the peace or sheriff must also be satisfied that one of the following conditions listed in *subsection (3)* is met:

- Admission to the premises has previously been refused;

- Admission is likely to be refused without a warrant;

- A search may be frustrated or endangered if immediate entry is not secured; and

- There is likely to be no-one present to grant admission to the premises.

769.   If a warrant is to be granted for reasons in subsection (3)(a) or (b), the justice of the peace or sheriff must be satisfied that notice of the intention to apply for a warrant has been given to the appropriate person (i.e. the occupier of the premises or the person with responsibility for their management).   Where no notice has been given, he must be satisfied that the giving of notice would seriously prejudice the purpose of the search.

770.   *Subsection (5)* provides that a warrant under subsection (2) will have effect for 28 days from the date of issue.

Section 307: Inspection of gambling

771.   A constable, enforcement officer or authorised person has the power to enter premises if it is reasonably suspected that facilities for gambling are being, are about to be or have been provided on the premises. This does not apply if the suspected gambling is private or non-commercial gaming or betting.

772.   This power to enter will apply for the following purposes: to establish whether facilities for gambling are, were or are about to be provided; to ascertain whether there is an appropriate licence in force; or to determine whether the terms and conditions of the licence are, have been or will be complied with.

Section 308: Operating licence holders

773.   A constable or enforcement officer has the power to enter premises where it is reasonably believed to be in use by the holder of an operating licence partly or entirely for purposes connected with the licensed activities. This provision is intended to provide a power of entry to premises where the gambling itself may not necessarily take place, but which are being used in connection with licensed activities, such as the head office of a business running a casino. A constable or enforcement officer may only exercise powers of entry under this section to determine whether the terms and conditions of the operating licence are being met.

Section 309: Family entertainment centres

774.   Where an application for a family entertainment centre gaming machine permit has been made, a constable, enforcement officer or authorised local authority officer may enter the premises for a purpose connected with the consideration of the application. Once the permit is in effect, the same may enter the premises to determine whether the gaming machines and the arrangements for their use comply with the requirements of the Act and any regulations made under it. Although constables, enforcement officers and authorised local authority officers have powers of entry under this section, it is anticipated that local authority officers will be primarily involved in the continuing inspection and enforcement of these types of premises. This is because it is the local authority which is responsible for issuing permits for these premises.

Section 310: Premises licensed for alcohol

775.   Part 12 and Schedule 13 make provision for Category C or D gaming machines to be made available on certain premises which are licensed to supply alcohol for consumption on the premises. This includes making gaming machines available under a licensed premises gaming machine permit. This section enables an enforcement officer or authorised local authority officer to enter premises in respect of which an application for such a permit has been made for a purpose connected with the consideration of the application.

776.   *Subsection (2)* specifies other circumstances in which a constable, enforcement officer or authorised local authority officer may enter premises which are subject to a licence to supply alcohol for consumption on the premises. Entry may be made to determine whether the gaming taking place satisfies the conditions for exempt gaming under Part 12; whether the terms and conditions of any relevant operating licence are being complied with where bingo is played on the premises; or whether section 281 applies (which is concerned with high turnover bingo). Entry may also be made to ascertain the number and category of gaming machines being made available for use on the premises.

Section 311: Prize gaming permit

777.   This section allows a constable, enforcement officer or authorised local authority officer to enter premises in respect of which an application for a prize gaming permit has been made. Once such a permit has effect, the same persons are

given the power to enter the premises to determine whether the prize gaming complies with the requirements of the Act or regulations made under it.

Section 312: Clubs

778.   This section allows authorised local authority officers to enter premises, where an application for a club gaming or club machine permit has been made, for a purpose connected with the application.

779.   The section also specifies the purposes for which a constable or enforcement officer may enter premises which are reasonably believed to be used by a members' club, a commercial club or a miners' welfare institute.   These are to determine whether gaming is taking or is about to take place, or whether any gaming that is or is about to take place is in accordance with the provisions for exempt gaming under Part 12, a club gaming permit or a club machine permit.

Section 313: Licensed premises

780.   This section gives the right of entry to a constable, enforcement officer or authorised person, to premises in respect of which an application for a premises licence has been made. This is to assess the likely impact of a licence being granted, in light of the licensing objectives. Once a licence is in force, there is also a power to enter the premises for a purpose connected with a review of the licence under Part 8.

Section 314: Lotteries: registered societies

781.   An enforcement officer or an authorised local authority officer may enter premises owned or used by a society registered with a local authority for the purpose of making inquiries about a lottery being promoted on behalf of the society.   It is likely that authorised local authority officers will primarily exercise this power to enter. This is because the local authority is responsible for the registration of societies under the provisions for registered society lotteries.

Section 315: Temporary use notice

782.   This section allows a constable, enforcement officer or authorised person to enter premises for which a temporary use notice has effect to determine whether the activities being carried on are in accordance with the terms of the notice. The right of entry will also apply where a notice has been given, but before it has effect. This will enable an assessment to be made of the likely effects of the premises being used for this purpose, in the light of the licensing objectives.

Section 316: Authorisations: production on demand

783.   This section allows a constable or enforcement officer to require an operating licence holder who has given a written authorisation, or the person to whom the authorisation has been given, to produce a copy of the authorisation. Failure to comply, without reasonable excuse, is an offence. The maximum penalty for the offence is a fine not exceeding level 2 on the standard scale.

784.   The types of authorisation which can be demanded under this section are:

- In relation to a pool betting operating licence, where the licence holder has authorised a person to accept bets on his behalf on a horserace course or dog track;

- In relation to a pool betting operating licence where the licence authorises the provision of facilities for football pools, where the licence holder has authorised a person to receive payments or entries on his behalf;

- In relation to a pool betting operating licence where the licence authorises horserace pool betting, where the licence holder has authorised a person to provide facilities for horserace pool betting; and

- In relation to a casino premises licence, where the licence holder has authorised a person or persons to use that premises for providing betting, bingo or both.

Section 317: Powers
785.   This section sets out the powers which a constable, enforcement officer or authorised person may exercise when entering premises under this Part.

786.   Those exercising powers of entry may inspect any part of the premises and any machine or other thing on them. There is also power to question any person on the premises, to access any written or electronic record on the premises, and to request copies. Those entering will also have the right to seize and retain material, but only where the person entering believes that it contains or constitutes evidence of an offence under the Act or a breach of licence conditions. Through regulations the Secretary of State will have the power to set rules concerning the treatment of copies of written or electronic records supplied, and items removed as evidence of an offence (past or present) or breach of licence condition. Regulations may also include provision regarding the retention, use, return or destruction of items supplied or removed and the conferring of a right of appeal.

787.   Restrictions are imposed on the extent to which a person entering premises can have access to and seize records without a warrant. It is only where a record (whether written or electronic) relates entirely to the matters to which the power of entry relates that it can be accessed or seized without a warrant. This is dealt with in further detail below in the note on section 319.

788.   A constable, enforcement officer or authorised person when exercising powers under this Part is not entitled to take any action in relation to anything of a kind specified in section 9(2) of the Police and Criminal Evidence Act 1984 (for example, legally privileged material). This restriction only applies in England or Wales.

789.   A constable, enforcement officer or authorised person must have regard to any relevant provision of a code of practice under the Police and Criminal Evidence Act 1984 in exercising any powers under this Part. This requirement does not apply in

Scotland.

Section 318: Dwellings

790.   A person exercising a power of entry under this Part may only enter a dwelling where authorised to do so by judicial warrant. A justice of the peace or the sheriff in Scotland may only issue a warrant if he is satisfied that, but for the requirement for a warrant, the person would be able to enter the premises in reliance on a provision of this Part. The justice of the peace or sheriff must also be satisfied that one of the following conditions listed in *subsection (3)* is met:

- Admission to the premises has previously been refused;

- Admission is likely to be refused without a warrant;

- A search may be frustrated or endangered if immediate entry is not secured; and

- There is likely to be no-one present to grant admission to the premises.

791.   If a warrant is to be granted for reasons in subsection (3)(a) or (b), the justice of the peace or sheriff must be satisfied that notice of the intention to apply for a warrant has been given to the appropriate person (i.e. the occupier of the premises or the person with responsibility for their management). Where no notice has been given, he must be satisfied that the giving of notice would seriously prejudice the purpose of the search.

792.   *Subsection (5)* provides that a warrant issued under this section is to have effect for 28 days from the date of issue.

Section 319: Records

793.   A person entering under this Part may only inspect or seize records (whether written or electronic) without a warrant where the records relate entirely to the matters to which the power of entry relates. Where records also contain information which is not relevant to those matters (i.e. where they are "mixed" records), then they may only be inspected or seized under the powers in *paragraphs (c) to (e)* of section 317(1) under the authority of a judicial warrant. For example, "mixed" records may contain information relating to personnel matters or may be commercially sensitive material irrelevant to the matters for which the powers of entry have been exercised. A justice of the peace may only issue such a warrant if he is satisfied that it is necessary to allow inspection of mixed records. The justice of the peace must also be satisfied that one of the following conditions is met:

- Notice has been given to a person in control of the records of the intention to apply for a warrant, or

- The purpose of exercising the power may be frustrated or seriously prejudiced by the giving of such a notice.

Section 320: Timing

794.   A power under this Part can only be exercised at a reasonable time. Reasonable time may depend on the circumstances. If the reason for the entry requires it to be made at a time that would generally be perceived as an unreasonable time, then that time might nevertheless be reasonable in the circumstances of a particular case.   For example, in a case where the person making the entry suspects that an offence is or is about to be committed and there is a strong likelihood that any evidence of the offence will be lost if entry is not made during night time hours.

Section 321: Evidence of authorisation

795.   An enforcement officer or authorised person wishing to exercise a power under this Part is required to produce evidence of identity and authority to a person (if there is one) who appears to be occupying the premises or to have responsibility for their management.

Section 322: Information

796.   This section requires the Secretary of State to make regulations about the information to be provided by those entering premises in reliance on a power under this Part. The regulations are to make provision about the nature of the information to be provided.   They are also to prescribe the form and manner in which the information is to be provided, the person to whom it is to be provided and the timing of its provision. *Subsection (3)* imposes a duty on a constable, enforcement officer or authorised person exercising a power under this Part to comply with any relevant provision of regulations made under this section.

Section 323: Use of force

797.   A constable has the authority to use reasonable force to enter premises when exercising powers under this Part. An enforcement officer has the authority to use reasonable force to enter premises where the entry is because he suspects that an offence under the Act has been, is being or is about to be committed on the premises. An authorised person or enforcement officer has the authority to use reasonable force to enter premises if he suspects that gambling (other than private or non-commercial gaming or betting) is taking place.

Section 324: Person accompanying inspector, &c.

798.   This section allows a constable, enforcement officer or authorised person to be accompanied by others when exercising a power to enter premises under this Part.

Section 325: Securing premises after entry

799.   A constable, enforcement officer or authorised person who enters premises under this Part is required to take reasonable steps to ensure that premises remain as secure as they were when they entered.

Section 326: Obstruction

800.   This section makes it an offence to obstruct or fail to cooperate with a constable, enforcement officer or authorised person exercising a power under this

Part. For example, it will be an offence to block the doorway to premises where an enforcement officer has requested entry. The maximum penalty for the offence is a fine not exceeding level 3 on the standard scale.

PART 16: ADVERTISING

801.   Part 16 makes provision relating to the advertising and promotion of gambling.

Section 327: Meaning of "advertising"

802.   This section sets out what it means to advertise gambling for the purposes of the Act. The definition is very broad and covers anything which is done to encourage people to take advantage of facilities for gambling (*subsection (1)(a)*). It also covers bringing information about gambling facilities to people's attention with a view to increasing the use of those facilities (*subsection (1)(b)*). As well as covering the activities of those who act with the specific intention of encouraging the use of facilities for gambling as described in *subsection (1)(a) and (b)*, the definition also provides for the advertising of gambling to include those who participate in or facilitate such activities. Advertising includes entering into arrangements such as sponsorship or brand-sharing agreements.

Section 328: Regulations

803.   This section gives the Secretary of State power to make regulations controlling the form, content, timing and location of advertisements for gambling, including requirements for specified words to be included in advertisements. A specific duty is imposed on the Secretary of State to have regard to the need to protect children and other vulnerable persons from being harmed or exploited by gambling. This reflects the licensing objectives of the Act concerning the protection of children and vulnerable people. Regulations under this section will apply to advertising by both "remote" means (such as email or television) and "non-remote" means (such as a poster on a hoarding or a magazine page). Specific provision about this is made in subsequent sections in this Part.

804.   It is an offence under this section to contravene a requirement of the regulations and any person guilty of an offence shall be liable on summary conviction to imprisonment for a term not exceeding 51 weeks (6 months for Scotland), a fine not exceeding level 5 on the standard scale, or both. An offence committed under this section shall be treated as a continuing offence which means that an offence shall be committed on each day during any period that the regulations are contravened.

Section 329: Broadcasting

805.   There are restrictions on the extent to which regulations controlling the form, content, timing and location of gambling advertisements, under this Part, may make provision about broadcast advertising. In particular, *subsection (1)* of this section prohibits the regulations under section 328 from making provision about advertising

by means of television or radio services to which section 319 of the Communications Act 2003 (c.21) applies. This is broadly a reference to those broadcast television and radio services which are subject to regulation by the Office of Communications ("OFCOM") under Part 3 of that Act. Section 319 imposes a duty on OFCOM to set, and from time to time to review and revise, standards for the content of programmes to be included in television and radio services.

806. *Subsection (2)* requires OFCOM to set, review and revise standards for the advertising of gambling under section 319 of the Communications Act 2003. The standards must reflect the provisions of regulations controlling the form, content, timing and location of advertising of gambling made under this Part. OFCOM must also consult the Commission before setting or revising the standards.

807. *Subsection (4)* ensures that all broadcast television and radio services of the BBC do not fall within the scope of regulations controlling the form, content, timing and location of advertising of gambling made under this Part. This includes the BBC World Service which is not to any extent a service to which section 319 of the Communications Act 2003 applies.

Section 330: Unlawful gambling
808. This section makes it an offence to advertise unlawful gambling. For these purposes, advertised gambling is unlawful if it requires a licence, notice, permit, registration or exception under this Act ("a licence etc."), in order for the gambling to take place without an offence under the Act being committed, and arrangements for the licence etc. have not been made at the time of advertising, or the exception does not apply to the arrangements. Take, for example, facilities for casino gaming which require operating, personal and premises licences to be obtained in order that the gaming can be provided without an offence being committed. Unless the necessary licences have been obtained at the time of advertising, any advertising of the gambling will constitute an offence under this section. The offence covers advertising of unlawful gambling whether the advertising takes place by remote or non-remote means, and sections 332 and 333 make specific provision about this.

809. The offence does not apply to lotteries. Part 11 of the Act contains separate provisions relating to the advertising of unlawful lotteries.

810. A person who commits the offence by doing anything to encourage people to gamble, or bringing facilities for gambling or information about them to the attention of others with a view to increasing their use, will have a defence if they can show that they reasonably believed the gambling to be lawful. People who commit the offence by participating in or facilitating such an activity will only commit the offence if they know or ought to have known the gambling to be unlawful.

811. There is also an exemption from this offence for peoples who advertise gambling because they merely deliver, transmit, broadcast or make data available in the course of business, without having any editorial control over the nature or content

of the material.

812.   A person guilty of an offence under this section shall be liable on summary conviction to imprisonment for a term not exceeding 51 weeks for England and Wales (6 months for Scotland), a fine not exceeding level 5 on the standard scale, or both. An offence committed under this section shall be treated as a continuing offence which means that an offence shall be committed on each day during any period that the advertisement is displayed or made accessible.

Section 331: Foreign gambling

813.   This section makes it an offence to advertise non-EEA (or "foreign") gambling. Foreign gambling is gambling which either physically takes place in a non-EEA state (e.g. a casino in Australia), or gambling by remote means which is not regulated by the gambling law of any EEA state (the interpretation section in Part 18 defines "EEA state"). For the purposes of this section, Gibraltar is treated as if it is an EEA state, which will allow gambling operators based in Gibraltar to advertise their services in the United Kingdom. The offence covers advertising of gambling whether the advertising takes place by remote or non-remote means, and sections 332 and 333 make specific provision about this. This section extends to Northern Ireland.

814.   The offence does not apply to lotteries. Part 11 of the Act contains separate provisions relating to the advertising of foreign lotteries.

815.   It will be open to the Secretary of State, however, to make regulations specifying countries or places which are to be treated as though they were EEA states for the purposes of this section. The effect of this will be to put any advertising of gambling taking place in that country or place outside the scope of the offence.

816.   The maximum penalty upon conviction for an offence under this section is a term of imprisonment of 51 weeks in England and Wales (6 months in Scotland and Northern Ireland), together with a fine up to level 5 on the standard scale.

Section 332: Territorial application: non-remote advertising

817.   This section clarifies the application of Part 16 where the advertising is by non-remote means, for example a poster on a hoarding.

818.   Where the advertising is by non-remote means:

- regulations controlling the form, content, timing and location of advertising under this Part; and

- the offence of advertising unlawful gambling under this Part;

will only apply where the advertising takes place wholly or partly in Great Britain; and:

- the offence of advertising foreign gambling under this Part,

will only apply where the advertising takes place wholly or partly in the United Kingdom.

Section 333: Territorial application: remote advertising

819.   This section clarifies the application of these provisions where the advertising is by remote means, for example by email or television broadcast.

820.   For remote advertising of gambling to fall within the scope of Part 16 it has to satisfy three tests. In the case of section 331 (the remote advertising of foreign gambling), it is only the first of the three tests which has to be satisfied. Furthermore, in the case of foreign gambling, the references to Great Britain in the first test should be read as references to the United Kingdom, because section 331 extends to Northern Ireland.

821.   The first test is broadly that the advertising must be targeted at people in Great Britain. In particular the advertising must involve:

- providing information intended to come to the attention of a person in Great Britain;

- sending a communication intended to come to the attention of a person in Great Britain;

- or making data available with a view to its being accessed by a person in Great Britain or in circumstances where that is likely to happen.

822.   The second test applies in the case of advertising that is either broadcast by television or constitutes an information society service within the meaning of Directive 98/34/EC (on electronic commerce). Information society service means "any service normally provided for remuneration, at a distance, by means of electronic equipment for the processing … and storage of data, and at the individual request of a recipient of a service".

823.   Where the advertising is broadcast by television the provisions of Part 16 will only apply if the broadcaster is either under the jurisdiction of the United Kingdom for the purposes of Directive 89/552/EEC (Television Without Frontiers) or is not under the jurisdiction of an EEA state for the purposes of that Directive. The purpose of this particular test is to ensure that the provisions do not apply to advertising where the broadcaster is properly regulated by another EEA State.

824.   Where the advertising constitutes an information society service, the provisions of Part 16 only apply where the service provider:

- is established in the United Kingdom for the purposes of Directive 2000/31/EC,

- is established in a non-EEA state for those purposes, or

- has been notified that the conditions for derogation in Article 3(2) of that Directive have been satisfied in relation to the service provider.

825.   Directive 2000/31/EC is concerned with contributing to the proper functioning of the Internal Market by ensuring the free movement of information society services between Member States. In broad terms the Directive establishes that a provider of information society services is to be regulated by the State in which it is established. Therefore, in general, where advertising constitutes an information society service, the provisions of Part 16 only apply where the provider is either established in the United Kingdom or outside the EEA. Article 3(4) of the Directive enables Member States to derogate from this general rule where the provider of an information society service not established in its country presents a serious and grave risk in respect of public policy matters such as the protection of consumers. The possibility to derogate under Article 3(4) of the Directive is also reflected in the section.

826.   The third test is that the gambling itself takes place in Great Britain where it is non-remote gambling; or, where it is remote gambling, that at least one piece of remote gambling equipment is situated in Great Britain.

PART 17: LEGALITY AND ENFORCEMENT OF GAMBLING CONTRACTS

827.   This Part deals with the legality and enforcement of gambling contracts. As a result of the sections in this Part, contracts made for gambling purposes are to be treated similarly to other contracts. In particular, any debts that arise from gambling will be capable of enforcement in the same way as any other personal or business debts. All statutory provisions which prevented such contracts from being enforced are repealed by the Act. However, the Commission is given power to void betting contracts in certain circumstances. These powers (set out in this Part) are intended to promote the licensing objectives (under Part 1) and enable the Commission to take specific action if it is satisfied that a bet was substantially unfair.

Section 334: Repeal of provisions preventing enforcement
828.   This section repeals all statutory provisions which provide that gambling contracts are unenforceable. The repeals will not apply retrospectively, so any gambling contract made, or right arising from an agreement made, before this section comes into force will not be enforceable.

Section 335: Enforceability of gambling contracts
829.   This section expressly provides that a contract will be capable of being enforced irrespective of the fact that it is a contract relating to gambling. This does not, however, override any other rule of law that prevents enforcement on the grounds of unlawfulness. Therefore gambling contracts may be void on the same basis as any other contract (for example, on the basis of lack of intention, mistake or illegality).

Section 336: Power of Gambling Commission to void bet

830.   This section provides the Commission with the power to make an order that a bet accepted by, or through, the holder of a general betting operating licence, a pool betting operating licence, or a betting intermediary operating licence, is to be void.

831.   Where the Commission exercises this power, any contract or other arrangement relating to the bet will be void, and any money paid in relation to the bet must be returned to the person who paid it. So, for example, a person who places a stake on a bet that the Commission orders should be made void, must have their stake returned to them. Equally, any winnings must be repaid to the person who accepted the bet. Such repayments will be enforceable as a debt.

832.   The Commission may only make an order under this section where it is satisfied that the bet was substantially unfair. In considering whether a bet is substantially unfair, the Commission must, in particular, have regard to any of the factors listed in *subsection (4)* that apply. These are:

  • that one or both of the parties to the bet (whether they made or accepted the bet) supplied information in connection with it that was insufficient, false or misleading;

  • that one or both of the parties to the bet believed, or ought to have believed, that the race or event about which the bet was made was, or would be, conducted in contravention of the industry rules (as defined in section 337(7)) that apply to the event. This might apply where, for example, one party to a bet knew that players in a youth football match were in fact over the legal age for participation, but nonetheless offered a bet on the match;

  • The fact that one or both of the parties to the bet believed, or ought to have believed, that the offence of cheating (as set out in section 42) had been, or was likely to be, committed in relation to the bet. This could apply where, for example, a person connected to a racehorse owner became aware that the horse had been deliberately injured prior to a race in which it was to run and, on the basis of that knowledge, made a bet on that horse through a betting intermediary;

  • The fact that one or both parties to the bet have been convicted of the offence of cheating as set out in section 42 of the Act.

833.   The effect of this section is that the Commission will not automatically void a bet where one of the factors listed in subsection (4) applies; it will only cancel a bet where it is satisfied that it was substantially unfair. This will allow for the situation where both parties to the bet knew about the cheating, for example, and so no unfairness arises.

834.   The power to void a bet will be available to the Commission for a period of six months from the day on which the result of the bet is determined, except where there has been a conviction for cheating, in which case there is no time limit. Provision is

made in section 337 for rights of appeal in relation to orders made by the Commission under this section.

Section 337: Supplementary

835. *Subsection (1)* of this section provides for a right of appeal to the Gambling Appeals Tribunal where the Commission makes an order to void a bet. Either party to the bet, and any other person who was a party to a contract or arrangement relating to the bet, will be able to appeal. This means that, for example, betting intermediaries who may lose money as a result of a bet being void, but who are not a party to the actual bet, are provided with a right of appeal. Further provision is made about the Gambling Appeals Tribunal in Part 7 of the Act.

836. *Subsections (2)* and *(3)* give the Commission power to void any part of a betting transaction, and to determine the consequences for any bets connected with a bet or betting transaction that is made void. Such a determination might, for example, require all the successive bets in an "accumulator" bet to be made void.

837. When investigating whether to order that a bet should be made void, the Commission may require any person by or through whom the bet is made or accepted (such as a party to the bet or a betting intermediary), to provide information or documents in relation to the bet. A person who does not comply with this requirement commits an offence, unless they have a reasonable excuse. The penalty for the offence will be a maximum fine of level 2 on the standard scale. In conducting its investigation, the Commission may also take into account any other information that it receives.

Section 338: Interim Moratorium

838. The Commission will have the power to make an order freezing any obligation to pay money in relation to a bet, where it suspects that it may need to make an order that the bet is void under section 336. The effect of this interim moratorium is to protect any payments that would otherwise have been made in relation to a bet, but which might be difficult to recover if the Commission later decides that the bet should be made void. So, whilst the interim moratorium is in place, a betting operator need not pay a customer any winnings; and the customer will not be required to pay any stake or commission.

839. The Commission need not be certain that a voiding order will be made before imposing the interim moratorium.

840. An interim moratorium will last for a period of 14 days, beginning on the day that it is made. It will be possible for the Commission to extend an interim moratorium by a further period of up to 14 days. There is no limit to the number of interim moratoriums that the Commission may impose in relation to any bet, although the time limit of 6 months for making an order to void a bet will continue to apply during any period when an interim moratorium is in place.

841.   The Commission may cancel an order for an interim moratorium before it expires; and must cancel one if it ceases to think that it might want to make an order to void the bet.

842.   Where the Commission decides to impose an interim moratorium, but then decides not to void the bet, the Commission will not be liable to make any payment (such as interest on the payments that have been frozen) simply because it has taken such action.

PART 18: MISCELLANEOUS AND GENERAL

843.   Part 18 contains a number of miscellaneous provisions. It provides powers for transitional arrangements to be made for implementation of the various new licensing and permit regimes established by the Act. It covers matters such as application of the Act to the Crown, and the prosecution powers of licensing authorities. It sets out a comprehensive interpretation section, and it provides for repeals and consequential amendments and the general extent of the Act.

Section 339: Prize competitions
844.   Participating in competitions in which there is a prize is not to be regarded as gambling as long as the activities involved in the competition do not amount to betting, gaming or participating in a lottery as defined in the Act.

Section 340: Foreign Betting
845.   This section repeals sections 9 to 9B of the Betting and Gaming Duties Act 1981 (c.63), which imposes prohibitions on certain activities relating to overseas betting, for the protection of the revenue. The provisions of Part 16 will provide a complete regime for the regulation of advertising, and as a result, these sections of the 1981 Act are no longer required.

Section 341: Offence committed by body
846.   If a body (such as a company) commits an offence under the Act, persons of authority in the body (known as officers) may be prosecuted if the offence resulted from their consent, connivance or their negligence. The body may be prosecuted also. Officers can include directors, managers, secretaries and members of a body. Where a body is a partnership then each partner is individually responsible for offences arising in these circumstances. Unincorporated bodies and their officers may also be prosecuted in the same way.

847.   *Subsection (7)* allows the Secretary of State to make regulations dealing with the application of this section to bodies formed outside the United Kingdom.

Section 342: False information
848.   Any person giving false or misleading information to the Commission or to a licensing authority, without a reasonable excuse, commits an offence. If convicted, the

person may be imprisoned for up to 51 weeks in England and Wales, or 6 months in Scotland, and may also be fined an amount up to level 5 on the standard scale. If the Commission or a licensing authority have taken a decision on the basis of false information they may do whatever in their judgement is necessary to alter or remedy the effects of that decision.

Section 343: Value of Prize

849.   This section is concerned with determining how the value of a prize is to be calculated. A number of provisions in the Act give powers to the Secretary of State to prescribe the maximum value of a prize that may be won at gambling. This section allows such regulations to include provision for determining what is meant by the value of a prize, where they are non-monetary prizes.

850.   *Subsection (3)* authorises a practice commonly known as "trading-up". This is where a person who has won two or more separate prizes from a gaming machine can swap the prizes won for another, different, prize. In the exchange, the value of the prize received must not be greater than the total value of the prizes that could have been won by the player from his winning turns on the machine. Thus, if a person wins two small toys from a Category D machine (and the maximum value of each prize is £8 under the Category D classification), then the two small toys can be swapped for one big toy provided the value of the big toy does not exceed £16 (2 x £8 prizes). The swap must also comply with any rules about the nature or type of prize that could have been delivered by the machine.

Section 344: Participation Fees

851.   This section provides a definition of "participation fee" for the purposes of the Act. Under various Parts of the Act, powers are taken to prescribe maximum participation fees for gambling (e.g. under Parts 5 and 12), or participation fees are prohibited in relation to certain forms of gambling (e.g. private gaming under Part 14). This section describes the matters which may or may not count as a participation fee. It gives the Secretary of State power to provide that a membership subscription is to be treated as a participation fee, as an exception to the general rule set out in *subsection (1)*.

852.   *Subsection (4)* allows the Secretary of State to deal with the apportionment of participation fees where the fee covers both gambling and non-gambling activities. An example of when this could be used is where a participation fee limit is set for the admission charge to premises where gambling takes place (see subsection (1)(b)), but some of that sum is referable to non-gambling activities. In such circumstances the fee could be apportioned, and only the gambling element of it limited. This power applies to all participation fee powers under the Act.

Section 345: Forfeiture

853.   Courts may order the forfeiture of items, like gaming machines, which are involved in the commission of offences under the Act. Items will be surrendered to the police. Persons who have not been convicted may make representations about any

items that are the subject of a forfeiture order, where they believe they have an interest in the article, and the court may order that the article be given to that person.

854.   It will be an offence to fail to co-operate with a forfeiture order, the maximum penalty upon conviction being a maximum term of imprisonment of 51 weeks in England and Wales, or 6 months in Scotland, and/or a fine up to level 5.

Section 346: Prosecution by licensing authority

855.   Local authorities have general powers to prosecute and defend legal proceedings, but this section provides power for them to institute proceedings with respect to specified offences under the Act. The section identifies those matters for which licensing authorities have express power to prosecute. This section does not apply to Scotland.

Section 347: Prosecution: time limit

856.   This Section disapplies section 127(1) of the Magistrates' Courts Act 1980 (c.43). That section limits the time for bringing a prosecution in the Magistrates' court to six months from the date upon which the offence was alleged to have been committed. *Subsection (1)* imposes a longer time limit, of 12 months from the date upon which the offence was alleged to have been committed.

Section 348: Excluded premises

857.   The Act generally applies to gambling on any premises in Great Britain, including vessels and vehicles. However, this Section provides an exception to this general provision by excluding from the Act premises which are subject to a national security certificate, issued by the Secretary of State or the Attorney General, or premises which are otherwise of a kind specified by the Secretary of State by order.

Section 349: Three-year licensing policy

858.   Licensing authorities perform a number of different functions under the Act. They issue premises licences under Part 8, temporary use notices under Part 9, and a range of permits, under Parts 10, 12 and 13 and Schedules 10, 12, 13 and 14. To assist them in this task, and to provide transparency for those wishing to apply to a licensing authority for a permission under the Act, all authorities are required to prepare a licensing policy, covering all their functions.

859.   This section sets out the procedures authorities must follow in preparing such a policy. Following widespread consultation, licensing authorities will publish a licensing policy statement describing the principles they intend to apply in exercising their various functions. The policy will have effect for three years, but the authority may review and alter the policy during that period. Regulations may be made by the Secretary of State (or Scottish Ministers in relation to Scotland) about the form of statements, the procedure to be followed in relation to them and their publication. An order of the Secretary of State will fix the first day of the initial three year period.

Section 350: Exchange of information
860.   Part 2 of the Act contains provisions which enable the Commission to exchange information with the bodies listed in Schedule 6. This section allows the bodies listed in Part 1 of that Schedule to exchange information amongst themselves for use in the exercise of a function under the Act. It also allows those bodies to provide information obtained in the course of functions under the Act to Her Majesty's Customs and Excise. The provision of information under this section may be made subject to conditions.

Section 351: Power to amend Schedule 6
861.   This section confers power on the Secretary of State by order to amend the lists of bodies in Schedule 6. In particular, it allows entries to be added to or removed from a list, and for entries to be moved from one list to another.

Section 352: Data protection
862.   The Act contains various provisions enabling bodies, including the Commission, to provide information to other organisations. This section makes it clear that nothing in the Act is to be taken as authorising a disclosure of information which would contravene the Data Protection Act 1998 (c.29).

Section 353: Interpretation
863.   This section provides the general definitions and meanings of expressions for the Act. Particular definitions of substance, in *subsection (1)*, are provided for:

- Director;
- EEA State;
- Football pools;
- Premises;
- Stake;
- Track (and dog tracks and horse-race courses);
- Vehicle; and
- Vessel.

864.   *Subsection (2)* contains a number of interpretative provisions for references in the Act. *Subsection (3)* provides a definition of what is meant by "virtual game, race or other event or process", and *subsection (4)* covers what is meant by giving notice under the Act.

Section 354: Crown application
865.   The Act applies to the Crown, which includes government departments and crown servants. However, the Act has no effect in relation to anything done on premises occupied by the armed forces.

866.   *Subsection (3)* ensures that a reference to "fire and rescue authority" in the Act will be substituted with a reference to "Her Majesty's Fire Inspectorate" in relation to premises for which Her Majesty's Fire Inspectorate is the proper fire authority. In particular, in respect of those properties for which they have responsibility, Her Majesty's Fire Inspectorate will be a responsible authority under Parts 8 and 9 and will be required to be notified of any application for a premises licence in relation to those premises.

Section 355: Regulations, orders and rules

867.   This section contains provisions governing the form and procedure for regulations, rules and orders made by the Secretary of State (or the Lord Chancellor) under the Act. Similar provision is made for regulations made by Scottish Ministers.

868.   Most **regulations** made under the Act are to be made by statutory instrument, pursuant to the negative resolution procedure. However, *subsection (4)* lists particular regulation-making powers which must be made pursuant to the affirmative resolution procedure (where made by the Secretary of State) or be approved by resolution of the Scottish Parliament (where made by the Scottish Ministers). **Orders** (with the exception of those listed in *subsection (7)*) are to be made by statutory instrument subject to the affirmative resolution procedure. By virtue of *subsection (8)* commencement orders under section 358 are not subject to any Parliamentary procedure except as provided in that subsection.

Section 356: Amendments and repeals

869.   As a result of the substantive provisions in the Act, there need to be consequential amendments made to provisions in other legislation and repeal of other Acts, in part or in their entirety. This section lists the major enactments repealed by the Act.

870.   *Schedule 16* contains the minor and consequential amendments arising from provisions of the Act. The minor amendments in Part 1 of Schedule 16 include amendments to the Gaming Act 1968. The amendments relate to the provisions of that Act concerned with gaming and gaming machines in premises licensed to supply alcohol. They also affect premises licensed under that Act, including in particular casinos. The amendments to the 1968 Act will apply until the repeal of that Act by this Act. *Schedule 17* lists provisions repealed by the Act, and the extent of their repeal.

Section 357: Money

871.   This section makes provision for expenditure and receipt of sums by a Minister of the Crown under the Act.

Section 358: Commencement and Schedule 18

872.   This section makes provision for the commencement of the Act. It provides for the preceding provisions of the Act to be brought into force by commencement order made by the Secretary of State. It is the Government's intention that the Act be

brought into effect in stages. This section makes this possible by allowing different parts of the Act to be brought into force at different times and in relation to different classes of activity under the Act.

873. *Subsection (2)(e)* specifically allows a commencement order to be made for the purposes of establishing the Commission so that it can carry out preparatory work prior to the repeal of the existing licensing regimes. *Subsection (2)(f)* makes it possible for provisions to be brought into force so that people who wish to provide facilities for gambling may make advance applications for a licence or permit under the Act, and for those advance applications to be considered and determined.

874. *Subsections (4) to (6)* enable savings, modifications and transitional arrangements to be made in the context of the Horserace Betting and Olympic Lottery Act 2004. This will enable provisions to be made that ensure the new licensing regime under the Act is compatible with that legislation.

875. This section and, in particular, *Schedule 18* provide powers to effect transition to the new regulatory regime and also allow effect to be given to what have become known as "grandfather rights". This means making provision whose effect is to require relevant authorities to grant new permissions to people making applications if they held equivalent permissions under the previous law.

876. Part 1 of Schedule 18 deals with the transitional continuation of old licences and permissions. In particular, *paragraph 3* allows particular provision to be made for casinos which are below the minimum licensable size, as defined by regulations pursuant to section 7 of the Act. This will allow such casinos to continue to operate, with controls, but without requiring them to meet the minimum size requirements.

877. Part 2 of this Schedule deals with advance and interim applications, and the need for licences to be converted from old licences to new licences in certain circumstances. The Government intend that these conversion powers will be used primarily in relation to applications for premises licences under Part 8, family entertainment centre gaming machine permits under Schedule 10, lottery registrations under Schedule 11, prize gaming permits under Schedule 14, and in relation to the gaming activities of clubs and pubs under Part 12. There is to be no automatic conversion for operating and personal licences.

Sections 359 & 360: Vessels and Aircraft: Territorial limitation
878. The Act applies to vessels and vehicles. See, for example, sections 211 and 231. Sections 359 and 360 establish the territorial limitation to the Act's regulation of vessels and aircraft.

Section 361: Extent
879. The Act applies to Scotland, England and Wales, but not generally to Northern Ireland. There are three exceptions to this. The offence of chain gifting in Part 3 and that of advertising foreign gambling in Part 16 apply to Northern Ireland, as does the

repeal of sections 9 to 9B of the Betting and Gaming Duties Act 1981 contained in this Part.

COMMENCEMENT

880.   The provisions of the Act (other than sections 358 to 362 which deal with commencement, territorial limitations, extent etc.) will be brought into force on dates appointed by the Secretary of State by commencement order. It has been the Government's intention to commence Part 2, which will provide for the establishment of the Gambling Commission, by October 2005. Schedule 16 includes amendments to the Gaming Act 1968 which will have effect until replaced by the relevant provisions of the Act. The intention has been also to bring these amendments into force at that time. Other provisions of the Act will be brought into force in stages after that with the intention that the Act should be fully in force by September 2007.

DETAILS OF THE BILL'S PASSAGE THROUGH PARLIAMENT

Parliamentary Stage	Date	Hansard Reference
House of Commons		
Introduction	18 October 2004	Vol. 425 Col. 658
Second Reading	1 November 2004	Vol. 426 Cols. 25 - 148
Committee	9 November 2004 – 16 November 2004	Standing Committee B
Introduction and Second Reading (New Session)	24 November 2004	Vol. 428 Col. 101-102
Committee	30 November 2004 – 11 January 2005	Standing Committee B
Report and Third Reading	24 January 2005	Vol. 430 Cols. 46 - 132
House of Lords		
Introduction	25 January 2005	Vol. 668 Col.1143
Second Reading	22 February 2005	Vol. 669 Col. 1136 - 1206

Order Motion	1 March 2005	Vol. 670 Col. 115
Committee	10 March 2005	Vol. 670 Col. 920 - 999
Written Statement	4 April 2005	Vol. 671 WS63 – WS76
Committee	6 April 2005	Vol. 671 Col. 822 - 874
Report and Third Reading	6 April 2005	Vol. 671 Col. 874
House of Commons		
Commons Consideration of Lords Amendments	7 April 2005	Vol. 432 Col. 1623 - 1631
House of Lords		
Lords Consideration of Commons Reasons	7 April 2005	Vol. 671 Col. 947 - 948

Royal Assent – 7 April 2005   House of Commons Hansard Vol. 432 Col. 1641

House of Lords Hansard Vol. 671 Col. 950

Printed in the UK by The Stationery Office Limited
under the authority and superintendence of Carol Tullo, Controller of
Her Majesty's Stationery Office and Queen's Printer of Acts of Parliament

4/2005   305995   19585